MW00824787

NATIVE AMERICAN NATIONS

VOLUME TWO

CREDITS

Writing
  Nigel D. Findley

Development
  Tom Dowd

Editorial Staff
  Senior Editor
    Donna Ippolito
  Assistant Editor
    Sharon Turner Mulvihill

Production Staff
  Art Director
    Dana Knutson
  Cover Art
    Jeff Laubenstein
  Cover Design
    Joel Biske
  Illustration
    Jim Nelson
    Janet Aulisio
    Larry MacDougall
    Tim Bradstreet
    Dana Knutson
    Mike Nielsen
    Jeff Laubenstein
  Layout
    Tara Gallagher
  Keyline and Pasteup
    Ernie Hernandez

Published by
FASA Corporation
P.O. Box 6930
Chicago, IL 60680

CONTENTS

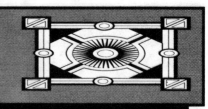

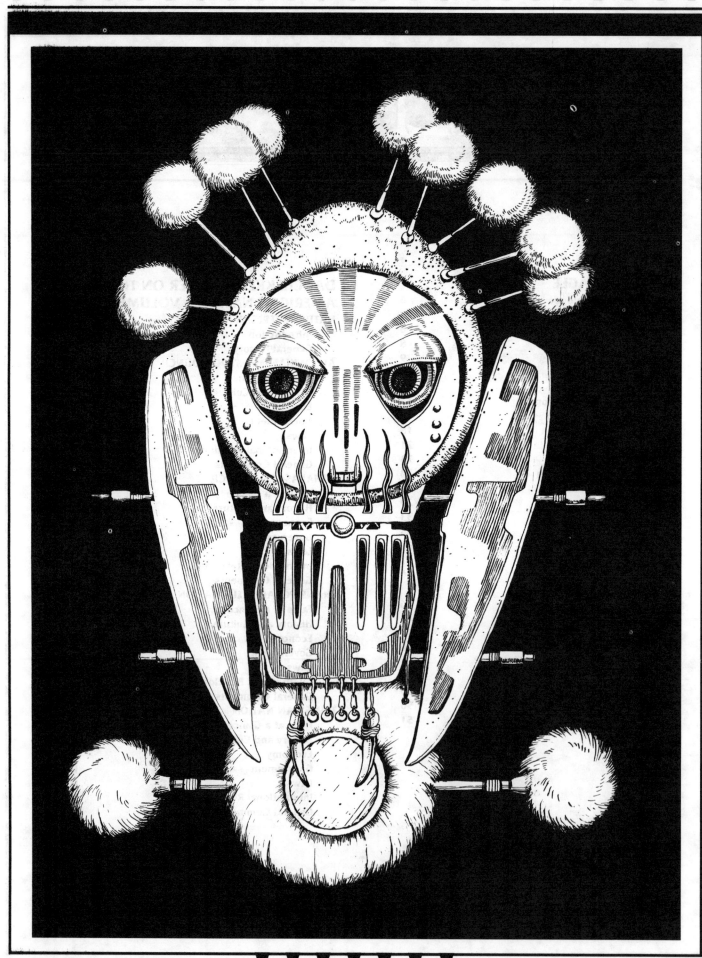

EYE OF THE EAGLE

They moved through the night, smoothly, silently. To David Tom, it seemed as if they were *part* of the night. Darkness embraced them, a comforting, almost tangible presence, shielding them from the eyes of those who would try to stop them. They were on the outskirts of a large town, Kemano, in the Tsimshian lands, but the skills he used now were the same ones he used in the woods, silent movement and observation skills he had learned hunting with his father. "Towns are just another kind of wilderness," the leader of his squad had said before they had left tonight, and he saw that to be true.

He paused at the corner of a building, searching the deserted street for enemies. He satisfied himself that the streets of this semi-industrial suburb were clear, and signaled the other members of his squad. They moved to join him.

There were twelve of them, all wearing black clothing, their faces dark with camouflage paint. David Tom and three fellow members of the Haida National Front had the lead, followed by the leader of the mission, a man named Wallace Blackwood. David Tom knew little about the hawk-faced, grim-eyed man other than that he was an important "field officer" with the Haida National Army of Liberation. Blackwood was flanked by what Tom had privately decided was his personal bodyguard of eight "hard men" picked from the ranks of the HNAL. Tom and the other two HNF members carried only hunting rifles, but the HNAL soldiers packed automatic weapons and had grenades slung on bandoliers crisscrossing their chests. Three of the soldiers also carried unknown cargo in heavy backpacks. Only Wallace Blackwood carried no obvious armament. But Tom had heard rumors that the man was a shaman of considerable power. If that was true, maybe he didn't need mundane weapons at all.

David Tom wondered again how he came to be on this mission. He was a Haida, one of the underclass in the Tsimshian Nation. For as long as his memory, his family and friends had suffered under the country's repressive regime run by members of the Tsimshian and Tlingit tribes. They denied his people access to higher education, and limited them to the lowest-paying manual labor. When he turned 18 two years ago, he had joined the Haida National Front, a political organization dedicated to combating governmental oppression of the Haida and Kwakiutl tribes. Its purely political nature was the only reason Tom had joined. As recently as five years ago the Haida National Front, or HNF, had engaged in actions far removed from political agitation, claiming responsibility for terrorist-style attacks that rocked the nation. The government's Peace Force struck back, virtually destroying the HNF and killing the vast majority of its leadership.

The survivors learned their lesson well: force would be met with force, fire with fire. They turned their efforts to education, political pressure, and spreading the word of governmental repression to other members of the Native American Nations, hoping that the Sovereign Tribal Council would take action. It did not.

Then the Haida National Army of Liberation arrived on the scene. Initially composed mainly of the few firebrands left in the HNF, the HNAL tried to force the older organization to "take up the sword" again, to fight the government with violence. They recruited the dissatisfied youth of the Haida and Kwakiutl tribes for their cause and orchestrated several minor bomb attacks.

The HNF quickly used its influence in the Haida community to try to control its violent offspring. For almost a year now, Tom figured, there'd been no bombings, nothing more violent than the occasional bit of minor sabotage, for which the HNAL quickly disavowed responsibility. The HNAL still staged penetration raids into government-run installations, mainly to leave warning graffiti telling the government that they could have taken out the place had they so wished, but nothing more.

This was their mission tonight. The last several months had appeared to bring a rapprochement between the leadership of the HNF and the HNAL. The HNF had even seconded members to the HNAL to take part in "graffiti raids," though Tom suspected it was mainly to make sure that nothing untoward happened. That's how he came to be under the command of Wallace Blackwood on this cold May night.

The target was less than three hundred meters away, a large electrical substation dead ahead of their position. This was a "distribution center" that took power from the nearby Kemano Aluminum Company's massive power house, stepped down the voltage, and fed it into the city's grid. (That was representative of much about Kemano, Tom thought. Just as the power that fed the grid was "spillage," power that the aluminum smelters didn't need, so was the city itself a side-product of the great metal processing plant on its outskirts. Without the smelter, Kemano would not exist.)

It was a good target. It nestled in a shallow bowl, surrounded by a residential neighborhood inhabited almost exclusively by Haida; who but Haida would live near something like that? Ringed by multiple fences and guarded by sensitive alarms, it was a perfect symbol of the governmentally sponsored abuse of the land and the underclass that was a way of life in the Tsimshian Nation. Penetrating the security would be hard, Tom knew, but it would be worth it. When the government saw the HNAL graffiti on the interior walls, when they realized that a few well-placed blocks of plastic explosive could have blown it sky-high, the knowledge that the Haida could no longer be safely ignored would once again be hammered home. Tom did not know the plan for the penetration, but Blackwood was unshakably confident about their chances for success. Perhaps the contents of the HNAL soldiers' backpacks would answer his questions.

The squad reformed on him at the corner, silent as wraiths. The building sheltering them looked down from the lip of the bowl directly above the substation, giving them a perfect view of the blocky installation. Tom checked the silent streets once more. Nothing stirred.

Soundlessly, Wallace Blackwood moved up to join him. "Good," the tall man breathed. "A fine position."

"When do we move in?" Tom asked. But Blackwood had already turned away. He signaled to his own troops. They swung their backpacks to the ground and quickly unpacked the equipment they contained.

It took David Tom a few seconds to realize what he was seeing. Then he recognized the blunt tube, targeting module, and the projectiles of a man-portable missile launcher. He turned to Blackwood, stunned.

The officer was smiling, a cold expression like the smile of a shark. "No graffiti tonight," he told Tom quietly. "Tonight we deliver a different message."

Tom's two HNF colleagues stared at Blackwood in disbelief, then looked away. Tom could almost hear their thoughts: "He's an officer," they were telling themselves, "we're just following orders."

But Tom pointed down the hill at the substation, at the small houses huddled against the protective wire. He knew the damage the missiles would do, could guess what would happen when they struck ultra-high-voltage transformers. "You can't," he hissed at Blackwood. "Our people are down there."

The big man stared calmly back at Tom. "The cause is just. A small price to pay, don't you think?"

Tom stiffened in disbelief. "*No*," he said fiercely. "Human lives are never a small price."

Blackwood considered him coldly. "You are under my command. Will you follow my orders?" His voice sounded casual, but Tom could hear the threat in his words.

David Tom took a deep breath before he replied, "I won't."

"I see," Blackwood whispered. He suddenly held a pistol, though he didn't seem to move. David Tom saw a flash, then his universe exploded into pain. He felt as if he'd been kicked in the head by a horse. The world spun crazily around him, then something hard slammed into his right cheek. As quickly as it had come, the pain was gone. He felt nothing, nothing at all. There was a rushing in his ears, the sound of a mighty wind or a great waterfall. Beneath the rushing sound was a deep, slow, booming, like the tolling of a great bell. His eyes were open: he couldn't close them, he couldn't move at all. He could see the electrical substation, still there but tilted at a drunken angle.

Something shot across his field of vision, hurtling like a comet or a shooting star, trailing flame and smoke. Whatever it was slammed into the substation building and burst into blinding light. Another explosion of light followed it, then another. Lightning arced up and out, dancing between the burning building and the metal fences surrounding it. Houses burst into flame like dry tinder. He heard running footsteps, fading away. Even through the roaring in his ears he could hear the screams.

Darkness rose around him, like a thick enveloping fog, and he fell headlong into it. As consciousness faded, he thought he heard wingbeats overhead. Wingbeats like those of a mighty eagle.

INTRODUCTION

Native American Nations, Volume Two is a sourcebook and roleplaying adventure set in the world of **Shadowrun**. The year is 2050. Astonishing advances in technology enable humans to blend with computers and travel through that netherworld of data known as the Matrix. Even more astonishing is the return of magic. Elves, dragons, dwarfs, orks, and trolls have assumed their true forms, while megacorporations (rather than superpowers) rule much of the world. North America has been balkanized into sovereign states, many occupied only by Native Americans ("Amerindians"). Moving through it all like whispers in the night are the shadowrunners. No one admits their existence, but no one else can do their secret work.

This sourcebook provides the gamemaster with background information on the Native American Nations, members of the NAN Sovereign Tribal Council. Each of the eight native nations is a unique society and culture, with its own eccentricities, strengths, and weaknesses. Each has its own world view, a place in the grand scheme of things, its own direction—and problems for those who run the shadows. **Native American Nations, Volume Two**, gives gamemasters the detailed background information they need to run adventures in the diverse tribal societies and to make these nations come alive for the players.

Native American Nations, Volume Two, also includes **Eye of the Eagle**, a complete roleplaying adventure that gives players the chance to interact with the inhabitants, governments, and other organizations of several tribal lands. In addition to being an entertaining adventure, **Eye of the Eagle** shows the gamemaster how the quirks of a culture can help create excitement and intrigue in a gaming session.

GAMEMASTERING NOTES

Eye of the Eagle uses a decision-tree format, allowing the players' team to arrive at encounters via various routes, depending on the choices they make. Their choices could also allow them to bypass a planned encounter. To run the adventure, the gamemaster needs a thorough familiarity with the contents of this book as well as a working knowledge of the basic **Shadowrun (SR)** rules. The contents of the adventure section of this book are for the gamemaster's eyes only, except for certain items earmarked as handouts for the players. (The players may, however, read the sections on the different Amerindian nations. After all, they would have access to this information through the local Shadowland bulletin board.) Everything needed to roleplay **Eye of the Eagle** is included here.

Eye of the Eagle is designed for a party of four to eight player characters. The group should contain a variety of talent, including at least one shaman and one decker. Combat skills will be very important for achieving a successful run.

Some encounters in this adventure are thoroughly planned out and described in detail. Others merely set the scene and remain open-ended. Hints for gamemastering each encounter style are included with the individual adventure sections.

MAKING SUCCESS TESTS

During the course of the adventure, the players will make a number of Unresisted Success Tests using a skill and a given target number. These Unresisted Success Tests will be indicated by the name of the appropriate skill and the target number. For example, a Stealth (4) Test would mean an Unresisted Stealth Success Test with a Target Number of 4.

SUCCESS TABLES

At times, the gamemaster will use Success Tables to determine how much information the players receive from various sources. Each Success Table lists different information for different numbers of die roll successes. Unless otherwise noted, the player should receive all the information for the level of success he rolled, as well as all the information for lower levels of success. For example, a character achieving 3 successes would receive the information for 3 successes as well as the information for 1 and 2 successes.

All animals have a natural Unarmed Combat skill equal to their Reaction.

HOW TO USE THIS BOOK

Aside from the basic **Shadowrun** rules, this book includes everything needed to play this adventure. However, certain magics used in **Eye of the Eagle** are more fully explained in **The Grimoire**, the **Shadowrun** magic sourcebook, and so the gamemaster may want to refer to that source for help in running this adventure.

The gamemaster should read through the entire adventure before beginning the game. Some important plot developments will not become apparent until well into the adventure, but the gamemaster will have to lay the groundwork early on. He can only do that successfully by being familiar with the storyline.

The gamemaster should also examine the maps, plans, and diagrams found throughout **Eye of the Eagle**, especially the floor plans of the various buildings. He should also read through the sourcebook sections for the Tsimshian Nation and the Algonkian-Manitoo Council in order to become familiar with the atmosphere and "texture" of each nation. This information will be useful when roleplaying inhabitants and officials of the nation in question.

The **Plot Synopsis** is a summary of both the story background and the course the adventure was designed to follow.

Eye of the Eagle begins with the section entitled **Farseer**, which offers suggestions for how to get the ball rolling and draw the characters into the adventure. The adventure follows, and is divided into short sections describing each of the encounters that the players will face, or are likely to face, in the course of roleplaying **Eye of the Eagle**.

Most of the encounters begin with text entitled **Tell It To Them Straight**. This should be read verbatim to the shadowrunners. It describes where they are and what is happening to them, as seen through their eyes. The gamemaster should adjust these descriptions to reflect the situation the characters are actually in, based on their previous actions. As always, adapt the situation given to move the action forward; do not try to force the player characters into a situation simply because the narrative describes only that situation. Special instructions to the gamemaster are printed in **boldface** type.

The information section, **Behind the Scenes**, is the real story. Only the gamemaster knows what is really going on at any given moment in an adventure. If a map is needed to play this encounter, it appears in this section. Stats for minor non-player characters needed to roleplay the section are usually included here, though the gamemaster may also be directed to existing Archetype or Contact statistics from the **Shadowrun** rule book or the **Sprawl Sites** sourcebook.

Each section ends with hints for the gamemaster in **Debugging**. These notes are suggestions for getting the story back on track if things go too far wrong. This section also suggests how to deal with player characters who get discouraged, and how to prevent the characters getting killed off too easily. The gamemaster may, of course, feel free to ignore these hints and let the chips fall where they may.

Legwork contains the information the player characters can obtain through their contacts or through the public data nets.

The **Cast of Shadows** provides principle non-player character descriptions and stats.

Picking Up the Pieces wraps up the loose ends of the adventure and includes tips on awarding Karma. The final section provides newsnet items to be used as handouts for the players, depending on the outcome of the adventure.

PREPARING THE ADVENTURE

It is impossible to create a published adventure that provides the appropriate opposition level for every diverse group of player characters. Some groups are inherently or effectively more powerful than others.

It falls then to the gamemaster to adjust the game statistics and capabilities of the opposition to provide an appropriate level of difficulty for the group. If the adventure does not suit the strengths and weaknesses of the player characters' group, the gamemaster can use it as an outline, the bones of an adventure that he will develop on his own. Or, if it works well except for a quirk here and there, he can change any part of the plot and events of the story that will make the adventure a better one for his players.

PLOT SYNOPSIS

The government of the Tsimshian Nation has always oppressed the members of two of the major tribes, the Haida and the Kwakiutl. Not surprisingly, a resistance network formed to fight this oppression. The center of this network was a group calling itself the Haida National Front, or the HNF. At first, the HNF fought oppression by peaceful means, conducting a political campaign against the government. Against the wishes of its founder, however, it soon became involved in acts of terrorism against the government, bombing Tsimshian police force facilities, industrial installations, and the like. The Tsimshian military reacted predictably: they came after the HNF with guns blazing, killing a good percentage of the group's members. The surviving HNF officers sensibly decided that violent opposition was not the way to go, and returned to using less direct methods.

Some HNF members disagreed. They considered political opposition totally useless. The only way to make the government take notice, they decided, was to kick where it would hurt. A group of firebrands broke away from the HNF and formed the Haida National Army of Liberation, or the HNAL. (Historically, this echoes the division between the Irish Republican Army and the Provisional IRA (the "Provos"), who split over the concept of senseless "public-relations" violence. Even the extremist Provos split when that group's hotheads, calling themselves the INLA, decided it would be wiz to bomb a couple of NATO radar installations.)

The leader of the HNAL is a Haida activist named Daniel Sheemahant, a young man respected by his comrades as an astute warrior and a dedicated enemy of the Tsimshian government. His lieutenant is also Haida, a man by the name of Wallace Blackwood. These two men are leading the HNAL on a new spree of violence against the powers-that-be in Tsimshian.

The HNAL is not alone in its war against the nation's government. The organization called TerraFirst!, often called "TF," has joined the fray. TerraFirst! has a history of successful eco-terrorism against California Free State. The northern arm of TerraFirst!, which has joined the HNAL, is currently led by a woman known only as Marta, a shaman of great power and personal magnetism. Marta and her group have joined with Sheemahant and the HNAL to aid in the destruction—or at least the disruption—of the Tsimshian government.

Though Sheemahant remains the nominal leader of the HNAL, it is known among the group's senior members that he is under Marta's influence. Nobody knows if this influence is personal, sexual, or magical. Initially, Sheemahant's targets were carefully chosen to inflict damage on important government installations while avoiding civilian casualties. Marta's influence has changed this. The last few exploits of the combined HNAL-TerraFirst! effort have killed a significant number of innocent bystanders. The most recent attack was a rocket strike against an electrical substation that killed many Haida and Kwakiutl residents of a neighborhood of Kemano. Many people elsewhere in North America, including members of the NAN Sovereign Tribal Council, do not realize that the HNAL and the HNF are different organizations. News of this latest rash of violence is further destroying the credibility of the HNF as a peaceful political movement.

More serious trouble is on the way. Sheemahant and Marta somehow learned of a secret research lab that the United States had built at the turn of the century near Klawock on Prince of Wales Island, which lies in what used to be Alaska and is now the Tsimshian Nation. When the United States military was forced to pull out of the area, they detonated explosive charges intended to completely destroy the underground lab. As it turned out, some of the charges did not go off. Instead of obliterating the lab, the explosion only collapsed parts of it, including the access tunnel. Sheemahant and Marta uncovered the intact portions of the lab, where they found some particularly nasty chemical and biological weapons that they now plan to use against the Tsimshian government.

At one time Sheemahant could not even have conceived of using such weapons of mass destruction. Under the influence of Marta, however, he looks forward to trying out his new toys. Marta knows these weapons are what she has been seeking much of her adult life.

Marta is a Toxic shaman, an Avenger. Like all Toxic Avengers, her personal agenda comes from the spirits to which she owes her powers. Her goal is to wipe out all human life in the Tsimshian region in retaliation for the government's shameless abuse of the land's natural resources. The chem-bio weapons from the secret lab are the perfect weapon for her plans.

The runners join the struggle through the efforts of a unique being. They are visited in Seattle by a woman, actually an eagle shapeshifter, calling herself Farseer. Farseer is aware of Sheemahant's activities and wants them to stop. For several reasons, she cannot go to the Tsimshian government, and nobody else will believe her story. Independent shadowrunners

are her last resort. She hires the players' team to discover exactly what Sheemahant and Marta are up to, and then to intervene before matters go too far.

From this point on, events are determined largely by the player characters. One possible scenario follows.

On their way to Kemano, the team just manages to avoid getting themselves blown up when an HNAL strike team missiles a bridge to smithereens. The team recovers quickly, capturing and interrogating one of the HNAL soldiers. He tells the team about a tavern in Kemano, The Randy Sasquatch, that serves as a meeting place for low-level HNAL members like him.

When the runners visit The Randy Sasquatch, they realize that one of the patrons, a man named Nightingale, is an HNAL recruiter. Accosting him, they discover that the HNAL uses a "store-and-forward" type voice-mail system to disseminate information among its members. They extract the number from Nightingale.

Decking into the Tsimshian local telecom grid, the team discovers the physical (street) address of the voice-mail number while fending off attacks from the HNAL and TerraFirst! They reach the deserted office building containing the voice mail system…

And run into an ambush. After first acquiring the physical voice-mail system—it is impossible to deck into it—the team must fight its way out through a gauntlet of HNAL snipers to safety. Breaking the security on the voice-mail system, they learn that Wallace Blackwood, a high-ranking HNAL officer, is on his way to a weapons lab in Klawock to pick up the remaining canisters of the bioweapon that Marta discovered.

The team hurries to Klawock, and meets up with Blackwood and his soldiers in the corridors of the underground lab. Defeating the goons, the runners learn from Blackwood that the HNAL has an operations base just over the border in the Athabascan Council. They also plunder the lab's computer system and find out more about the bioweapon Marta is using, a nasty war virus code-named Red Masque.

On their way to the Athabascan Council, they hear a newscast about a "dead zone," a place where all mammalian life appears to have been killed off, located near their destination. Sounds like Marta's been testing her viral toys.

The team has a run-in with a go-gang that seems a bit off its feed. From what the team learned from the lab's computer system, they realize that these go-gangers have been infected by Red Masque. From the gangers, they learn the exact location of the HNAL base.

The base is deserted when they arrive, but they discover a computer storage chip that someone left behind. The chip shows the deck plans of the TMV Queen of the North and a position reference from a nautical chart. Checking the public databases, the runners learn that the Queen of the North is a ferry running from Port Hardy in the Salish-Shidhe nation to Kitimat, the capital of Tsimshian. The chart reference represents a location along the ferry's course. This information leads them to conclude that Marta and Sheemahant plan to load the Red Masque virus onto the ferry and sail it into Kitimat harbor, killing countless thousands of people.

They quickly acquire transportation and catch up with the ferry, which has been hijacked by HNAL troops, just as Marta and even more troops are loading the viral bombs aboard. In a hard-fought battle, they defeat Marta, Sheemahant, and the HNAL goons. Will they also be able to destroy the viral bombs?

FARSEER

TELL IT TO THEM STRAIGHT

The good old Blue Flame Tavern never seems to change, you say to yourself as you jander in the door. The same smoke-filled atmosphere—courtesy of several interesting substances burning in various pipes—the same torn vinyl seats and scarred plastic tabletops, the same in-your-face razorboys and girls looking you over with meat or electronic optics. The credit from your last score is almost gone, but the rep you and your chummers picked up remains. It's obvious by the speed with which the Flame's regulars look away. That's satisfying. But satisfaction won't buy you drinks, and the balance on your credsticks won't stand up to more than a couple of rounds of the tavern's watered liquor. Ah, well, that's why you came here. Biz always seems to find you at the Flame.

"Hoi, chummers." The barkeep greets you in his thin, strongly accented voice. A good-natured grin shows his lack of teeth. "Heard 'bout the score you pulled awhile back. Smooth moves, lotsa jammin'. First round on the house, ha?" Without waiting for an answer, he starts pouring your usuals.

Your grin broadens. When the Chinaman passes out free drinks early, it means he'll drop an extra charge onto your credstick later in the evening when he hopes you're in no condition to notice. Nothing ever changes at the good ol' Blue Flame.

You've taken your regular booth, and the free drinks are a warm glow in your bellies when the Chinaman appears at your table. "Looking for biz, ha?" The words are a question, but the tone is a statement. "Got something for you, maybe. Lady in the back." He gestures with a scarred thumb toward the private room at the rear of the tavern. "Real looker, too," he leers, "but kinda scattered. Says she wants some talent." He winks. "Offered her my kinda talent, but think she wants younger stuff. Told her to wait, knew you'd be in later. Saved her for you, ha?"

You smile again. Like drek the Chinaman "saved her for you." You just happened to be the first team with any kind of rep that wandered in here tonight. But you nod appreciatively, knowing there will be a hefty "service charge" when you pay your tab.

"Wanna go see her?" the Chinaman asks. "She waiting for you."

The bartender knows nothing more about the "looker" than he's already said. If the team decides to visit the back room, read the following.

The Chinaman thumbprints the lock. It's sophisticated tech for a sleazy tavern, but that's the Blue Flame for you. The door swings open and you jander in.

The Chinaman was right: the woman is a looker. A hair under two meters, you guess, massing around 63 kilograms, and all of it in the right places. Long, silver-white hair and golden skin, with a strong, aquiline nose, and piercing dark eyes. There's something strange about those eyes. They're steady and wise, but there's something else there as well: confusion, maybe, or fear. They are, you decide, the eyes of someone who's very much out of her element.

"You are shadowrunners?" she asks, her voice powerful and sharp. You can imagine that voice screaming in anger or exhilaration. (Now where did that thought come from?)

The woman doesn't wait for your answer. "My name is...Farseer," she says, "and my home is the land you call Tsimshian. I came to the city because my home is in danger. No one in Tsimshian can help me. My need, the land's need, is great.

"The land is in grave danger," she continues. "As I understand it, a group is trying to unseat the government by causing destruction and death. Normally, the ways of governments and of people do not concern me. But I have learned that this group has now acquired a means to devastate the land, to kill all living things that dwell on or above the earth. And that does concern me. You must help me," she says earnestly, "you must remove this threat to the land."

She pauses. "I learned much of this from a human who was called David Tom. I learned it from him before he died. He was unable to tell the group's name to me in full. The only word he spoke was 'Haida.' This Haida group will cause irreparable harm to the land unless you stop them. Will you do this?"

Gamemaster's Note: Farseer's answers to the runners' questions appear in "Behind the Scenes." She will not volunteer information about her true nature.

If the runners broach the subject of payment, read the following.

"Yes," the woman says speculatively, "I suspected that you might ask for reward. I can offer you something now, and my word as a..."—she hesitates—"...my personal word that you will receive ten times this measure, should you complete the task. Will this be sufficient payment?" She reaches inside her coat, which you notice is feather-trimmed, and extracts an irregularly shaped object.

It's a chunk of something, bigger than her fist, and it shines dully in the florescent light. She hands it to you—and you almost drop it. It's much heavier than something that size should be. Unless it's...no, it couldn't be. A nugget of gold that size? It must be worth a couple of thousand nuyen at the very least. And the woman promised you ten times that if you complete the mission.

If one of the runners assesses Farseer's true nature and challenges her with it, read the following.

"Yes," Farseer says simply. "I am an eagle, one of those your kind calls a shapeshifter. Now you will understand the high regard in which I hold the land, and the importance I attach to stopping this threat against it."

BEHIND THE SCENES

The character who calls herself Farseer is far different than the Mr. Johnsons the runners are used to dealing with. She is not human or even metahuman: she is an eagle shapeshifter (**SR**, p. 187). This explains some surprising gaps in her knowledge, and her naiveté when it comes to humans. She will not volunteer information about her true nature, but will acknowledge it freely if she is assensed and challenged with the truth. See **Cast of Shadows**, p. 49, for further information on Farseer, including some hints on how to roleplay this meeting.

Farseer will tell the runners as much of the truth as she knows. The unfortunate David Tom was unable to gasp out much information before he expired: only that a group called the Haida-something is stepping up its campaign of violence in its attempt to unseat the Tsimshian government. From spirit sources, Farseer has learned that a group, presumably the same one, has gained access to an agent of mass destruction that poses a great threat to the land. (In fact, this "agent of mass destruction" is a chemical-biological weapon, but the nature spirits that Farseer deals with would neither know nor use those words.) All she knows is that this group now has the capability to blot out virtually all life wherever they choose to attack.

Farseer has little understanding of human and metahuman thought processes and philosophies. The puzzles of government, civil insurrection, and terrorism are a closed book to her. She cannot comprehend them, and thus will be unable to answer the runners' questions about the Haida group's actions or intentions. All she knows is that they pose a terrible risk to her land and must be stopped.

The runners may request that the eagle shapeshifter accompany them on the mission. Farseer categorically refuses. If pressed, she will admit that something about the Haida group deeply disturbs her, a feeling she can neither explain nor ignore. She knows that she will not be able to get close enough to the Haida group to be of any help. (Farseer is sensing the Toxic nature of Marta.)

If the gamemaster wishes, Farseer can offer the runners the assistance of a powerful air spirit, someone or something she calls Tael (pronounced teel). She will hand them a leather pouch containing a small handful of owl feathers, and will tell the runners, "If you need my friend, scatter these on the breeze. Tael will feel them and come." If the runners demand a guarantee of its help, she will explain that other creatures of nature also fear for the land. Tael is one of these. Basically, Tael is a one-shot, "get-out-of-trouble-free," *deux ex machina* the player characters can invoke if things get out of control, particularly in **Over the Bounding Main**, p. 37. If stats are needed, Tael should be considered a Great Form Air Spirit of Rating 8 or 10. The gamemaster should try to avoid imposing any numbers on Tael unless absolutely necessary. Tael should instead be used as a tool to assist the runners one time during this adventure. When Tael is called, the character who loosed the feathers will hear a voice whisper in his or her ear, saying "What would you have me do?" The spirit will render this one service to the runners at the gamemaster's discretion.

If the runners ask Farseer for suggestions about where to begin, she will only reply, "This is not my area of knowledge. This is why I came to you." She can only tell them that she found the dying David Tom on the outskirts of the Tsimshian town of Kemano, in the middle of a burning neighborhood. (She does not know how the fire started, of course, or understand its signifi-

cance. The runners can easily discover that information if they do any digging in Kemano.) If they need a push, Farseer will suggest they start in Kemano. She cannot help them to get into Tsimshian or to Kemano; when it comes to entry papers and transportation, the runners are on their own. (See the **Tsimshian Nation** chapter, p. 93, for information on getting to and into Tsimshian.)

The nugget Farseer gives the runners is pure gold, worth 14,500¥. (Of course, fencing it might be a bit of a problem.)

The runners must find their own way into the Tsimshian Nation and north to Kemano. Arranging transportation and entry into the nation could develop into a mini-adventure in its own right. No bus transportation is available into Tsimshian, airlines are expensive (and get a bit twitchy about passengers with AK-97s as carry-on luggage), and the boat is slow. The runners will probably be much better off arranging for or "acquiring" private land transportation.

Once the runners are in Tsimshian, go to **Land of Hope and Promise**, the next section.

DEBUGGING

The runners may refuse to take the job—but then, any team that would turn down a lady in distress is a poor excuse for shadowrunners. If the runners balk, Farseer will plead with them a little, playing on their egos (she understands humanity that much). If they continue to be stubborn, she will walk away and look for another, more cooperative shadow team.

Particularly obtuse players might neglect to ask for such vital details as where David Tom was when he shuffled off this mortal coil. If so, Farseer will volunteer the information—preferably in a manner that brings home to the player characters what boneheads they are for missing the easy question.

LAND OF HOPE AND PROMISE

TELL IT TO THEM STRAIGHT

Gamemaster's Note: This encounter may be timed to more accurately reflect the means by which the runners enter Tsimshian. It can occur early in their travels or as they near their destination.

Judging by your first couple of hours in the nation, Tsimshian is a dreary, depressing place. There's heavy, slate-gray cloud cover, and the torrential downpour of cold rain hasn't let up since you crossed the border. You remember spotting a sign on the customs office at the border station. "Welcome to Tsimshian," it said, "Land of Hope and Promise." Yeah, right. Hope to get out of this place soon, and promise yourself never to come back.

At least Route 16 is in good condition—better than some of the highways around Seattle. Wet conditions make high speed rather risky, but at least there're no major potholes. The road is currently hugging the side of a steep river valley. The river below winds like a snake, and the road follows it. Which means you're always negotiating "suicide hairpins"—a rock wall on the right and a sheer drop thirty meters down to the river on the left. Nice.

Ahead, you see a bridge spanning the valley. The road looks pretty straight on the other side. Good. You'll be over the bridge in a few seconds, and then you can put the pedal down and make up some time.

Something crosses your field of vision from the right, a streak of light trailing white smoke. It impacts in the middle of the bridge with a violent explosion. Horrified, you see the center of the bridge disintegrate.

BEHIND THE SCENES

The bridge is the latest target of the HNAL. The Kemano substation strike was more sensational, but this is almost as significant: taking out this bridge cuts one of the major land routes to the Tsimshian capital of Kitimat.

The rocket causes a 20-meter-long segment of the bridge to collapse. When the missile detonated, the runners' vehicle was still far enough away to stop in time, but just barely. (The gamemaster may want to have the driver make a Skill Test, just to put a scare into the players, or even roll an impressive handful of dice. No matter what the result, the runners' vehicle screeches to a halt on the very lip of the precipice.)

A particularly militant team might decide to try to jump their vehicle over the gap. This is possible, but risky. The vehicle must be traveling at the speed of at least 100 meters per vehicular combat turn (p. 71, **SR**). If the vehicle is traveling any slower when it attempts the jump, it automatically fails, with the

catastrophic consequences described later. (This means runners trying to jump the gap in something like a Mitsubishi Runabout—with a top speed of 75 kph—are automatically out of luck.) Assuming the vehicle is traveling at 100 meters per vehicular combat turn or more, the driver must make a Car or other appropriate Skill Test against a Target Number of 5. See the following table for jump attempt results.

Successes	Result
0	Catastrophic failure. The vehicle plummets into the river valley. The crash has a damage category of Deadly and a Staging of 3. Driver and passengers must make a Resistance Test as if they had been hit by a weapon with a Damage Code of 3D2. (This is the outcome if the vehicle is traveling too slowly.)
1	Marginal success. The vehicle makes it across the gap, but still suffers damage. The impact has a damage category of Serious and a Staging of 3. Driver and passengers must make a Resistance Test as if they had been hit by a weapon with a Damage Code of 3S3.
2	Moderate success. The impact has a damage category of Light and a Staging of 3. Driver and passengers must make a Resistance Test as if they had been hit by a weapon with a Damage Code of 3M3. This is stun (mental) damage only.
3–4	Respectable success. The impact has a damage category of Light and a Staging of 3. Driver and passengers are totally unharmed.
5+	Spectacular success. The vehicle sails across the gap, landing smoothly. No vehicular damage results from the jump, and the passengers are not even shaken up.

If the runners decide not to try to jump the gap, they will have to backtrack and take another route. (While the time spent in backtracking has no game significance, the gamemaster should play up the inconvenience factor.) But before they can do so, another problem comes to their attention.

The HNAL team that took out the bridge is positioned on a ridge overlooking the road. Though they were not ordered to eliminate witnesses, they were not expressly forbidden to mess with anyone on the road. Unless the runners hightail it out of the area immediately, the HNAL goons will take potshots at their vehicle(s) with assault rifles from their position about two hundred meters away. (Fortunately for the runners, the HNAL team only had one missile.) Of course, they assume the vehicle(s) contain helpless tourists. As soon as they see a group of chromed, angry shadowrunners pile out, they turn and flee. The runners may pursue the team or let them bug out, as they see fit. The HNAL team comprises three soldiers and the gunner who fired the missile.

HNAL Soldier (Three)

The soldiers are Haida, members of an oppressed underclass. Their oppression does not change the fact that these individuals are thugs. Other people join the HNAL for philosophical reasons, but these boys signed on just so they could blow things up. Geeking harmless tourists is one thing; standing up to a bunch of in-your-face shadowrunners is something else. As soon as they find out who their opponents are, the soldiers bug out.

The HNAL goons have a four-wheel drive vehicle concealed up-slope from their position, ready for a quick getaway.

B	Q	S	C	I	W	E	M	R	Armor
4	4	5	2	2	3	6	—	3	None

Dice Pools: Defense (Armed) 1, Defense (Unarmed) 3, Dodge 4
Skills: Armed Combat 4, Car 2, Etiquette (Street) 2, Firearms 4, Unarmed Combat 3
Gear: AK-97 [Assault Rifle, 22 (clip), 5M3], Knife (2L1)

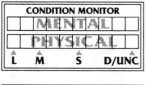

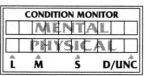

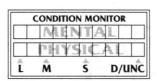

HNAL Gunner (One)

This guy differs from his fellows only in that he knows how to fire a man-portable rocket launcher.

B	Q	S	C	I	W	E	M	R	Armor
3	5	4	2	3	3	6	—	4	None

Dice Pools: Defense (Armed) 3, Defense (Unarmed) 2, Dodge 5
Skills: Armed Combat 3, Etiquette (Street) 2, Firearms 3, Gunnery 3 (Concentration: Missile Launchers 5), Unarmed Combat 2
Gear: Ares Viper [Heavy Pistol, 30 (clip), 4M2], Shoulder-fired Missile Launcher [no missiles available; as Club, +1 Reach, (Str + 1M2) Stun]

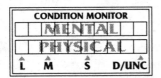

Ford Canada "Bison"

Handling	Speed	B/A	Sig	APilot
4/3	45/135 *	5/2	4	1

Seating: 2 bucket seats plus 2 folding bench seats
Access: 2 standard plus 1 cupola
* Off-road speed is 35/105. Engine is multifuel, but liquid fuel is only on stock models. Enclosed rear tray model is available for 165¥.

The slopes above the road are rugged and rocky, providing plenty of cover, but also slowing movement. The runners will have to push themselves to catch the goons before they make it to their vehicle.

The soldiers are new to the HNAL. In fact, blowing the bridge was their "initiation" into the group. They know very little about the organization. They were recruited from the slums of Kemano by a man called Nightingale who they met at a tavern called The Randy Sasquatch. He is their only contact in the HNAL proper, though they do know several other recruits like themselves. They do not know the name of the HNAL leader, are unaware of the group's involvement with TerraFirst!, and—obviously—have no clue to Sheemahant's (or Marta's) intentions. They are aware of the missile attack on the Kemano electrical substation (as described in the **Prologue**) and suspect that it was staged by the HNAL. In other words, the runners will not get much information from interrogating the goons, other than confirmation that the HNAL is active in Kemano and that The Randy Sasquatch might be a good place to start their research.

If the runners fail to capture any of the HNAL members, but do geek one, they can still pick up a clue pointing to The Randy Sasquatch. One of the dead HNAL soldiers has a cheap, multi-use, techno-match in his pocket with the tavern's name inscribed on it. If there is more than one dead body, the runners find the matchstick on the first body they search.

If the runners learn about The Randy Sasquatch and decide to take their investigation to the tavern, go to **Watering Hole**, p. 21. If they do not learn about the tavern, or if they want to do some other legwork before going to The Randy Sasquatch, go to **Welcome to Kemano,** the next section.

DEBUGGING

Unless the runners manage to splatter themselves on the valley floor, not much can go wrong here. (If the team is about to do something real dumb—and the gamemaster is feeling generous—he may give the driver of the vehicle a chance to realize the folly of his actions. If the team decides to ignore this hint, let the chips—and the runners—fall where they may.)

If the runners either geek the HNAL goons on the spot or let them get away, all is not lost. The only really significant piece of information to be gained in this encounter is the name of The Randy Sasquatch tavern, and the runners can pick up this knowledge later on.

WELCOME TO KEMANO

TELL IT TO THEM STRAIGHT

As you pull into the town of Kemano, the rain that held off for the past half-hour starts coming down again. Your first view of the town is a gray, cold, wet, drab, and depressing place…not unlike a smaller version of Seattle. You could almost feel at home here.

BEHIND THE SCENES

This section gives the runners an opportunity to work any contacts they can dig up in Kemano. They also need to find some kind of accommodation if they want to spend any time in town. Refer to the map on the next page for an idea of the layout of the town and the location of significant landmarks.

Kemano particularly, and Tsimshian in general, is not a hospitable place. To bring this fact home to the runners, the gamemaster should feel free to create several "nuisance encounters" with either Kemano police or the locals. The police patrol Kemano in pairs. Locals can accost the runners in groups of four to a dozen members.

Kemano City Police (Two)

A member of the Tsimshian or Tlingit tribe, the Kemano police officer is one healthy socioeconomic step above most of Kemano, and he fragging well knows it. Anglos and metahumans are one rung further down than the citizens of Kemano. While he might not have any real reason to roust visitors, he still enjoys rattling their cages a little. If they respond with force, he will gladly cut them down, or call up reinforcements who can handle the job for him.

B	Q	S	C	I	W	E	M	R	Armor
4	4	4	1	3	3	6	—	3	5/3

Dice Pools: Defense (Armed) 4, Defense (Unarmed) 2, Dodge 4
Skills: Armed Combat 4, Etiquette (Street) 4, Firearms 3, Police Procedures 3, Unarmed Combat 2
Gear: Armor Jacket (5/3), Micro-transceiver (police and emergency frequencies only), Stun Baton (+1 Reach, 5L2 + Special), Uzi III [SMG, 16 (clip), 4M3]

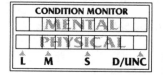

CONDITION MONITOR		CONDITION MONITOR	
MENTAL		MENTAL	
PHYSICAL		PHYSICAL	
L M S D/UNC		L M S D/UNC	

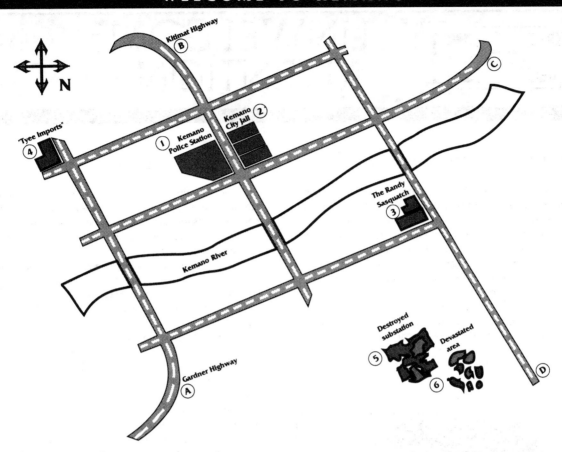

Aggressive Local (Four or more)

Haida or Kwakiutl, the locals are poor, oppressed, and chronically un- or under-employed. Not a happy camper, he or she takes pleasure from passing on a little abuse to the only people lower on the totem pole; visitors, particularly Anglo visitors. Violence is not the goal, but if the visitors show their teeth the locals will respond. (Even the stupidest local will think twice about messing with a group of chromed shadowrunners, however.)

B	Q	S	C	I	W	E	M	R	Armor
4	3	4	3	3	3	6	—	3	None

Dice Pools: Defense (Armed) 2, Defense (Unarmed) 3, Dodge 3
Skills: Armed Combat 2, Etiquette (Street) 4, Etiquette (Tribal) 3, Firearms 2, Stealth 1, Unarmed Combat 3
Gear: Streetline Special [Hold-out Pistol 6 (clip), 3L1], Knife (2L1)

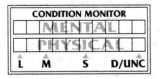
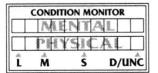
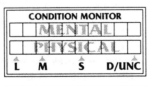

The runners should be somewhat discreet when looking for information here, remembering that information flows both directions on the street. Careless inquiries can send word back to the objective of those inquiries, and the runners could, at the least, lose the element of surprise.

If the gamemaster decides the runners' questions are too blatant, the HNAL will learn, much to their displeasure, that some strangers are looking for them. Go to **Unwelcome Attention**, the next section. If the team has learned about The Randy Sasquatch, go to **Watering Hole**, p. 21.

DEBUGGING

Experienced runners should realize by now that messing with any police force is a bad thing to do. The Kemano police can mobilize enough men, packing enough hardware, to take down just about any shadow team. While they will match any deadly force used against them, their standing orders are to arrest and incarcerate troublemakers for eventual trial. Only the runners can make them shoot to kill. If the runners force a confrontation and then get themselves caught, give them one chance to escape en route to the Kemano jail. Should they hose that chance, they deserve to experience the tender mercies of the Tsimshian justice system.

Trouble can come in two forms in this encounter. The players' characters can get themselves geeked by cops. The players can also be skunked in their information search by cold dice. The gamemaster can fudge the rolls and hand them some information to keep things rolling, or (for more fun), run the nasty encounter in **Unwelcome Attention**, the next section.

UNWELCOME ATTENTION

TELL IT TO THEM STRAIGHT

Gamemaster's Note: Run this encounter if the team, or individual members of the team, take to the streets of Kemano.

"Yo, Anglo!" a harsh voice yells as you pass the mouth of an alley. You and your friends turn as one to face the voice. There's one rough-looking hombre standing in the shadows. Amerindian, of course, and big enough to make an Urban Brawl player look malnourished. A suspicious bulge under his duster looks like some kind of heat.

"You been asking some nosy types of questions," he growls. "Not a good idea. There are some things enquiring minds don't want to know, you get my drift?" With an almost-inaudible snick, a scalpel-sharp spur extends from the man's forearm. He smiles nastily. "Better you should get the frag out of town, Anglo. Right fragging now."

BEHIND THE SCENES

The Amerindian in the alley is a minor lieutenant in the HNAL, a hard man everyone calls Jawbone. If the runners stay cool, he does too. He delivers his warning and then fades back into the shadows. The team can press the issue if it wants, but Jawbone came prepared.

Jawbone's backup is three heavies; Ghostwind (a shaman), Zack (street muscle), and Dretch (ditto), all of whom are currently invisible courtesy of Ghostwind. If the runners decide they want to party with Jawbone, the other three immediately join the festivities.

The HNAL members will hit hard, but they will also fight smart. If they think they can take down the runners, they give it their best shot. If it looks like they are overmatched, they will make a fighting withdrawal. They carry away their wounded or dead unless stopping to pull them out would be suicidal. In general, the foursome will err on the side of caution. After all, they came to deliver a message, not to get into a war.

The runners may end up with a prisoner to interrogate. Obviously, the HNAL member will not tell them anything willingly, but the runners can use magic or plain, old-fashioned physical intimidation to extract information. Any of these HNAL members can provide details on the HNAL itself, the Kemano raid, and The Randy Sasquatch, and will at least know the names of Sheemahant, TerraFirst!, and Marta. They know nothing about the weapons lab or Sheemahant and Marta's next move. The structure of the HNAL resembles the cells of the French Resistance Underground. Members know limited information, and so cannot give the whole organization away. Even Jawbone can only "betray" run-of-the-mill street muscle like Zack and Dretch. Contact between upper-eschelon members is limited to a voice-only phone number with a store-and-forward voice-mail system, a high-tech answering machine that lets users save and retrieve messages. Jawbone and other senior HNAL members phone in at least once a day to leave or retrieve messages. Both Jawbone and Ghostwind can provide this number, LTG# 2604 (24-6051). Neither know the system's physical location.

Anyone can leave a general message to be picked up by the system operator. To leave a confidential message for a particular person, the caller must use that person's single-word "mailbox identifier." A single word password (different from the mailbox identifier) retrieves messages from the personal mailbox. The mailbox identifiers of the major HNAL officers are their first names: Daniel, Wallace, Marta, and so on. Jawbone's personal password is "Freedom," and Ghostwind's is "Frag you."

Jawbone

A junior lieutenant in the HNAL, Jawbone is a tough piece of work, big and strong and sporting a serious attitude problem. Wallace Blackwood, his superior, ordered him to put a scare into the runners. (This was a bad idea, but Jawbone does not question orders.) Ordered to avoid confrontation if he can, he actually welcomes any opportunity to mess up the runners.

B	Q	S	C	I	W	E	M	R	Armor
6	4	6	3	3	3	5.7	—	3	5/3

Dice Pools: Defense (Armed) 5, Defense (Unarmed) 5, Dodge 4
Skills: Armed Combat 5, Etiquette (Street) 4, Etiquette (Tribal) 4, Firearms 5, Negotiation 3, Stealth 2, Unarmed Combat 5
Cyberware: Retractable Spur (right arm, 6M2)
Gear: Armor Jacket (5/3), Knife (3L1), Uzi III [SMG, 16 (clip), 4M3, Gas-Vent Stabilization (2)]

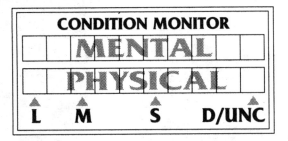

Ghostwind

A Grade 2 Initiate Shark shaman and a true believer in the Haida cause, he will do anything to further the HNAL's goals. When Ghostwind is wounded or kills an opponent in combat, he goes berserk for 3 combat turns and must make a Willpower Success Test with a Target Number of 6 (**Grimoire**, p. 108). Subtract one turn of berserker rage for each success rolled. His centering technique is pseudo-yogic posturing.

B	Q	S	C	I	W	E	M	R	Armor
4	5	3	4	6	6	6	6	5	5/3

Dice Pools: Astral Defense (as Skill), Astral Dodge 6, Astral Magic 5 (2), Astral Special 2, Defense (Armed) 3, Defense (Unarmed) 3, Dodge 5, Magic 5 (7)
Skills: Armed Combat 3, Conjuring 5, Etiquette (Street) 3, Etiquette (Tribal) 5, Firearms 3, Magical Theory 5, Sorcery 5, Stealth 2, Unarmed Combat 3
Gear: Amulet (Power Focus 2), Armor Jacket (5/3), Orichalcum Knife (Weapon Focus 3), Remington Roomsweeper [Heavy Pistol, 6 (cylinder) 4M2, w/Laser Sight]
Spells: Invisibility 5, Mana Cloud 3, Manablast 4, Powerblast 3, Stunblast 3
Totem: Shark

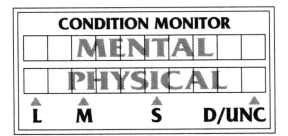

Zack

Zack got involved with the HNAL because his buddy and mentor Jawbone did. He is cunning, if not overly bright, and has an innate understanding of weaponry that makes him particularly useful to the HNAL leadership. He would follow Jawbone to hell and back and not ask questions.

B	Q	S	C	I	W	E	M	R	Armor
5	4	5	2	2	4	5.3	—	3	5/3

Dice Pools: Defense (Armed) 3, Defense (Unarmed) 4, Dodge 4
Skills: Armed Combat 3, Etiquette (Street) 2, Etiquette (Tribal) 2, Firearms 7 [Concentration: SMGs (9), Specialization: Uzi III (11)], Firearms B/R 5, Stealth 2, Unarmed Combat 4
Cyberware: Low-Light Eyes w/Flare Compensation, Smartgun Link
Gear: Armor Jacket (5/3), Knife (2L1), Uzi III [SMG, 16 (clip), 4M3, w/Built-in Smartgun Link and Recoil Compensation (2)]

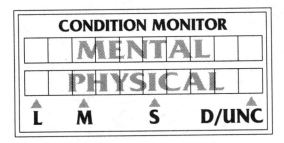

Dretch

Like Zack, but more so.

B	Q	S	C	I	W	E	M	R	Armor
6 (8)	3	6	1	2	3	1.3	—	2 (6) (+2D6)	5/3

Dice Pools: Defense (Armed) 3, Defense (Unarmed) 4, Dodge 3
Skills: Armed Combat 3, Etiquette (Street) 2, Etiquette (Tribal) 2, Firearms 5 [Concentration: Pistols (7), Specialization: Ares Predator (9)], Firearms B/R 2, Stealth 1, Unarmed Combat 4
Cyberware: Dermal Plating (2), Low-Light Eyes w/Flare Compensation, Smartgun Link, Wired Reflexes [(2) (+2D6 Initiative)]
Gear: Ares Predator [Heavy Pistol, 10 (clip), 4M2, Built-in Smartgun Link], Armor Jacket (5/3), Knife (3L1)

If the runners decide to visit The Randy Sasquatch, go to **Watering Hole**, the next section. If they acquired the phone number of the HNAL voice-mail system and decide to follow up on that angle, go to **Hold the Phone**, p. 23.

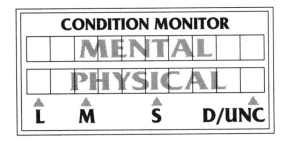

DEBUGGING

Though it might be a tough fight, a determined group of shadowrunners can survive a dustup with Jawbone and his chummers. If the runners acquire a live prisoner in the fight and interrogate him, they can learn a lot about what is happening.

Unfortunately for the runners, capturing one of the HNAL team is unlikely. The runners will probably geek one or more of the HNAL squad and find themselves interrogating a corpse. No problem. They can get back on track several ways. If the runners search a body, they will discover a matchstick from The Randy Sasquatch. If the dearly departed is Jawbone or Ghostwind, they might (at the gamemaster's discretion) find the HNAL voice-

mail LTG number scrawled on a piece of paper. (This latter option is a short-cut. Use it to save time and to by-pass The Randy Sasquatch if the players do not understand the tavern's significance.)

If the team let the HNAL goons get away, or the bad guys managed to drag their dead off with them, the clues are still available. If the runners have already heard about The Randy Sasquatch, leave well enough alone. If they do not know about the tavern yet, or if they discarded the information as irrelevant, have one of the runners notice something the HNAL team left behind: a matchstick from...you guessed it. (If the players or their team are being particularly obtuse, the HNAL voice-mail number may be scrawled on a matchbook cover.)

WATERING HOLE

TELL IT TO THEM STRAIGHT

As you jander in the door of The Randy Sasquatch, you have an incredible sense of deja vu. Smoke-filled air, torn vinyl seats and scarred plastic tabletops, hard-edged patrons glaring at you—this could be the Blue Flame back in Seattle.

But there the similarity ends. The Flame caters to metalled-up types like yourself and your chummers. Here, all customers are off the rack (but not pushovers), and obviously Amerindian.

There's a holo over the bar depicting the tavern's name-sake. All the male members of your team stare in unabashed envy for a moment. Then you get down to business.

BEHIND THE SCENES

Use the Bar location archetype from **Sprawl Sites**, p. 12.

This scene is an ideal opportunity for roleplaying. If the runners show proper respect and ask the right questions, they might discover valuable information. At the very least, they will learn that one of the locals in the bar is a low-level member of the HNAL. If they handle themselves badly, taking a page from Dale Carnagree's *How to Make Enemies and Alienate People* (apparently required reading for most shadowrunners) they will buy themselves no end of grief.

The gamemaster should remember that The Randy Sasquatch is in a bad part of town, making most of its patrons Haida or Kwakiutl; mean Haida or Kwakiutl, at that. Most residents of Tsimshian dislike Anglos. These guys dislike everybody, but reserve their blackest animosity for Anglos. No matter how tactful the runners are, it is likely they will antagonize at least one person. If the players' characters respond to this antagonism with violence, they will have a full-fledged barroom brawl on their hands. If the runners are too tactful, however, the locals might label them as wimps and decide to mess them up just on principle. The runners need to walk a fine line. Difficult, yes, but then nobody said this job was easy, did they, chummer?

Excluding Nightingale and the runners, eight customers currently have the run of the place. (Use the Human Pedestrian Contact from **Sprawl Sites**, p. 116, but increase Body and Strength to 4 and arm them with light personal weapons.) One bartender is on duty. (Use the Bartender Contact from **Shadowrun**, p. 163, and arm him with a sap and a Remington Roomsweeper. Hey—this is a tough bar.)

If the runners play it right, they can learn three things of importance:

•Yes, The Randy Sasquatch is sometimes frequented by very junior members of the HNAL.

•Though the locals support the goals of the HNAL, some worry privately that the group is getting out of control.

•The guy sitting at the end of the bar, a chummer called Nightingale, is a member of the HNAL.

The following table may be helpful for getting everyone involved in the roleplaying for this encounter. (See **Legwork**, p. 40, for how to run this table.)

BAR TALK

The following information is available from any habitué of The Randy Sasquatch.

Appropriate Contacts (Target Number 4)

Anyone at The Randy Sasquatch

Successes	Result
0	"Frag you, Anglo!" (The patron leaps to his feet, fists clenched, ready to kick some shadowrunner butt. Subsequent events depend on the team's reaction.)
1	"Get outta my face, you piece of drek." (The patron is antagonistic, but not immediately violent. If the runner wants to press the issue, the Target Number is increased by +2.)
2	"Leave me alone." (No information, but no open hostility, either. The runner can try again with no penalty.)
3	"Yeah, we get some HNAL types in here. At least, they claim to be members. I think they're just grunts and dumb street muscle, most of them."
4	"The HNAL? Yeah, I support what they're trying to do. Frag, we all do. But the way they're doing it…I dunno, it scares me, wondering what they're going to do next."
5+	"See that big-shouldered son-of-a-slitch at the end of the bar there? Nightingale he calls himself, or some such drek. He's the guy you should be talking to. He's HNAL, I know that for a fact."

The runners can handle Nightingale several ways. They can pretend they want to join the HNAL. Well, if they are not Amerindians, and if they have no chance of convincing him they are of Haida or Kwakiutl extraction, forget it. An Amerindian team member with a good line might be able to convince Nightingale to consider recruiting him, but that will not get the team anywhere either. Nightingale simply asks for a way to contact the "applicant," and says he will be in touch. ("Don't call us, chummer, we'll call you.") Dead end.

They can follow Nightingale and hope he leads them somewhere interesting. Nightingale stays at the tavern for about an hour, time enough for a couple of beers, then hits the road and janders back to his one-room apartment, where he holes up for a couple of days. (The HNAL wants him to keep his head down for awhile after the bridge incident.) Dead end.

Finally, they can confront him with his HNAL membership, either in the bar or on the street. Nightingale is one cool cobber, and will calmly deny his involvement with the HNAL. If the team pressures him, he will fight and try to escape. Nightingale is one of those "victory or death" types. A clever team may be able to keep him alive for interrogation, but he knows very little. Yes, he recruits for the HNAL, and is nominally a member. But the only senior member he knows is a guy who calls himself Jawbone, and he has no idea where that worthy personage can be found. His only contact with Jawbone or the HNAL is through the phone number LTG# 2604 (24-6051).

If the team wants to check out the LTG#, go to **Hold the Phone**, the next section.

Nightingale

Nightingale is one Haida who is mad as hell and not going to take it any more. He joined the HNAL hoping for the opportunity to go out and kick some Tsimshian and Tlingit butt. Unfortunately for him, the HNAL leadership decided that he did not measure up as a street soldier. He does have good people skills, however, so the organization placed him in recruitment. Though Nightingale recognizes the importance of his part in the revolution, he still harbors dreams of becoming "a soldier on the front line opposing the oppressors." If the runner team pushes him hard enough, he takes this chance to live out his dreams and gives the fight his all.

B	Q	S	C	I	W	E	M	R	Armor
3	3	3	6	4	4	6	3	—	4/2

Skills: Armed Combat 2, Etiquette (Street) 4, Etiquette (Tribal) 4, Firearms 3, Negotiation 3, Psychology 4, Stealth 1, Unarmed Combat 2

Gear: Beretta 101T [Light Pistol, 10 (clip), 3M2, w/Laser Sight], Knife (1L1), Lined Coat (4/2)

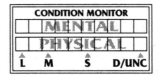

DEBUGGING

A particularly in-your-face team of shadowrunners might decide that a good, diverting barroom brawl is just the ticket. If that spins their crank, they are welcome to start it up. As long as combat remains non-lethal, that is, knuckles and knees, the tavern's clientele will join in with a will. Once the first weapon is drawn, or the first neck gets snapped, only the most militant locals will continue to party. The others will make their escape through a convenient door or window.

As soon as trouble starts, the bartender hits the PANICBUTTON under the bar. A squad of 10 Kemano Police (see **Welcome to Kemano**, p. 16, for stats) will arrive in 2D6 minutes. If the brawl has not escalated, they will respond with enthusiastic brutality but not lethal force. If lead is flying, however, they do whatever it takes to put a stop to it, including geeking anyone and everyone who looks dangerous. They will call up support squads as needed. If the runners are arrested, give them one chance to escape, and lock 'em away for a good long time if they miss this opportunity. (Getting the police involved is just plain stupid.)

The runners may get a little over-zealous and geek Nightingale before they get a chance to talk to him. If so, he should have the HNAL voice-mail LTG number on a scrap of paper in his pocket (sending the team to **Hold the Phone**, the next section). Should the team neglect to search his body, or if they lose him, run **Unwelcome Attention**, p. 18. If the runners have already dealt with Jawbone, go to **TerraFirst! at Last**, p. 27.

HOLD THE PHONE

BEHIND THE SCENES

The team can investigate the LTG number they found by calling it directly or decking into the phone system to discover its physical location.

If they call, a voice-mail system on the other end answers (voice only), "This is Tyee Imports. Please leave a message, or press star to send a fax." This is a cover, of course. Messages are picked up by the sysop (system operator) and dealt with appropriately. The voice-mail system also has sophisticated voice recognition software. If the runner making the call speaks the first name of one of the HNAL officers, Daniel, Marta, Wallace, and so on, any subsequent message is stored in that person's personal mailbox. If the runner speaks either Ghostwind's or Jawbone's password, which they might have learned in **Unwelcome Attention**, they hear a playback of a confidential message. For both individuals, the message is the same: "When you've dealt with the intruders, leave a status report here. I'll contact you later." The voice is Sheemahant's, though the runners have no way of knowing this. Dialing directly into the voice-mail system does not reveal its physical location.

Deckers cannot break into the voice-mail system electronically. The HNAL anticipated the possibility that their electronic security would be threatened, and eliminated the threat in a very simple way. They simply eliminated the direct electronic connection between the voice-mail system and the phone grid. When a call comes in, the phone automatically opens the line in "hands-free," or speaker phone, mode. The voice-mail system communicates with the phone by microphone and speaker. The system is archaic, yes, and it does degrade the sound quality somewhat (which could be a clue). But it effectively locks out the deckers. Anyone attempting to deck into the voice-mail system must make a Computer (4) Test. A single success tells them that decking into the system is impossible (explain the rationale stated above to the player). Zero successes on this roll means they do not discover that the task is categorically impossible. The decker believes his failure just means that he is not handling the intrusion correctly, or that the security is more serious than he thought.

Decking into the Tsimshian LTG to dig up the physical location of LTG# 2604 (24-6051) is easy. Since this penetration is fairly insignificant in and of itself, it can be handled in the abstract. (Individual gamemasters might disagree. Feel free to whip up a quick map of this corner of the Matrix and let the team's decker go at it. The Tsimshian grid has a security of Orange-5. The gamemaster may also use the Quick Matrix Resolution system presented in **Virtual Realities**, but even that level of simulation is unnecessary.)

For ease of play, assume that the decker moves from the SAN through which he entered to the appropriate datastore without any problem. Once there, he must defeat the security, which is Orange-5. This means the decker must score three successes against a Target Number of 5 to successfully download the physical location, that is, the street address, of LTG# 2604 (24-6051).

Gray Trace and Report IC lurks in the datastore. If the decker triggers the ice and fails to kill it, a team of eight Kemano police will arrive at the decker's physical location in ten minutes. (For the police, use the stats in **Welcome to Kemano**, p. 16.)

The street address of the LTG# is 115 N. Fifth Avenue. This is in the warehouse district—a particularly bad part of town, as the runners can easily discover. If they decide to follow up on this information, go to **The Dark Side of Town**.

DEBUGGING

The runners may fail to pick up the Fifth Avenue address; if so, other ways of getting them back on track appear later. The gamemaster can point them in the right direction immediately using several options.

First, if the runners have not yet visited The Randy Sasquatch, the right stimulus might persuade Nightingale to divulge the street address. See **Watering Hole**, p. 21, for details.

Option two is to shamelessly fudge the die rolls when the team tries to deck into the Tsimshian LTG. Let the decker sweat a bit—make him think that he is right on the hairy edge of triggering some nasty black ice—but give him the paydata no matter how cold the dice.

The next time the players' characters hit the street looking for information from their contacts, put the third option into play. Somebody tells the runners that the grapevine says HNAL owns an office at 115 N. Fifth Avenue.

THE DARK SIDE OF TOWN

TELL IT TO THEM STRAIGHT

Fifth Avenue in Kemano is a grimy warehouse district that's seen much better days. It reminds you of the Redmond Barrens—vacant lots here and there, condemned buildings, burned-out cars on the sidewalks. And there's the constant feeling that you're being watched by rodents, both the two-legged and four-legged varieties.

Surprisingly enough, 115 N. Fifth Avenue isn't a warehouse. It's a meeting hall of some sort, probably once used by a policlub. A sign still hangs over the door, but so many letters are missing that it reads T HN R Y. The front door and all the windows look like they were boarded up at one time, but the thrifty residents of this neighborhood seem to have requisitioned most of the ply-board for their own purposes.

If one of the runners scouts astrally, read the following.

You take a couple of deep, centering breaths, and slip out of your body. You move toward the building. Something leaps at your astral body!

It's a coal-black dog, its snarling face practically level with your throat.

BEHIND THE SCENES

Use the Policlub Meeting Hall archetype from **Sprawl Sites**, p. 32.

The HNAL figured the team would visit their voice-mail system and set up a brutal ambush. Seven HNAL soldiers, including a combat shaman and a sniper, are deployed around the building. They plan to let the team enter the building and experience the unpleasant surprise awaiting them, and then hose them down when they leave. The shaman brought her pet along with her, a trained hell hound named Poopsie.

The runners can enter the building by the front door or through a window, or run an astral check before they go inside. If the team heads in without scanning astrally, refer to the map in **Sprawl Sites**. If the team magician scopes out the building from the astral plane, Poopsie will pounce. Because Poopsie is a hell hound, a dual being trained for hunting on the astral plane, she senses when a team member goes astral and will follow her instincts by attacking immediately. The HNAL soldiers want to wait until the "surprise" in the office has softened the team up a little before they cut loose, but the shaman will attack if it looks as though her pet is in trouble and the rest of the soldiers will be forced to support her. Even if the HNAL soldiers must fight on someone else's agenda, they will fight smart, using the available cover to their best advantage. If they appear outclassed, the HNAL troops will attempt an orderly, fighting withdrawal, and will do their best to take their wounded and dead with them.

Even in this part of town, major fire fights are rare, and so attract the attention of the police. A squad of eight Kemano police in a Citymaster will arrive on the scene ten minutes after the first shot is fired. If high-velocity lead is still flying when they arrive, the police will shoot to kill anyone packing obvious weaponry.

If the runners manage to capture and interrogate one or more of their attackers, they learn the information also available in **Unwelcome Attention**, p. 18.

HNAL Soldier (Five)

More intelligent and better trained than the team that blew the bridge in **Land of Hope and Promise**, the HNAL soldier and his colleagues planned their ambush and know exactly how to coordinate the attack and withdrawal. Though far from suicidal, he is not afraid to risk his life to complete his mission.

B	Q	S	C	I	W	E	M	R	Armor
4	5	4	3	3	5	6	—	4	4/2

Dice Pools: Defense (Armed) 4, Defense (Unarmed) 3, Dodge 5

Skills: Armed Combat 4, Etiquette (Street) 4, Etiquette (Tribal) 4, Firearms 5, Stealth 2, Unarmed Combat 3

Gear: AK-97 [Assault Rifle, 22 (clip), 5M3, w/Shock Pads (1), and Built-in Smartgun Link], Armored Coat (4/2), One IPE Defensive Aerodynamic Hand Grenade (5S4), Knife (2L1), Micro-transceiver, Smart Goggles

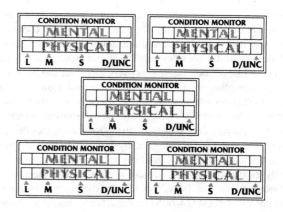

HNAL Sniper

Similar to his colleagues, this fellow is a specialist at long-range, one-shot take-downs. As such, he is less inclined to get down and dirty in hand-to-hand combat, preferring to stay well back and drop his enemies with a few accurately placed shots.

B	Q	S	C	I	W	E	M	R	Armor
4	5	3	3	4	5	6	—	4	4/2

Dice Pools: Defense (Armed) 3, Defense (Unarmed) 2, Dodge 5
Skills: Armed Combat 3, Etiquette (Street) 3, Etiquette (Tribal) 4, Firearms 4 (Concentration: Rifles 6; Specialization: Ranger Arms SM-3 Sniper Rifle 8), Stealth 4, Unarmed Combat 2
Gear: Armored Coat (4/2), Ranger Arms SM-3 [Sniper Rifle, 6 (magazine), 6S2, w/Imaging Scope (3) and Gas-Vent Recoil Compensation (3)], Micro-transceiver

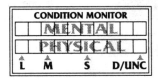

HNAL Combat Shaman

A typical Rat shaman, she prefers ambush to toe-to-toe combat, and is skilled at arranging situations to suit her fighting style. Her love for her pet hell hound can lead her to act uncharacteristically, however. If she thinks her pet is getting trashed, she will throw everything she has at the culprit, even if doing so leaves her open to counterattack.

B	Q	S	C	I	W	E	M	R	Armor
3	4	3	6	6	6	6	5		4/2

Dice Pools: Astral Defense (as Skill), Astral Dodge 6, Astral Magic 6, Defense (Armed) 2, Defense (Unarmed) 2, Dodge 4, Magic 5 (6/8)
Skills: Armed Combat 2, Conjuring 5, Etiquette (Street) 4, Etiquette (Tribal) 5, Firearms 3, Magical Theory 5, Sorcery 5, Stealth 3, Unarmed Combat 2
Gear: Defiance T-250 [Shotgun, 5 (magazine), 3M3, APDS], Knife (Power Focus 1), Micro-transceiver, Ring (Combat Spell Focus 2)
Spells: Clout 2, Confusion 4, Mana Dart 4, Mana Missile 4, Overstimulation 4, Power Dart 5, Power Missile 5
Totem: Rat

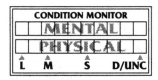

"Poopsie" the Hell Hound

Poopsie the hell hound is only half trained, and so will not obey commands in the heat of battle.

B	Q	S	C	I	W	E	R	Attack
4	4x4	5	—	3/4	3	(6)	6	6M2

Powers: Enhanced Senses (Improved Hearing and Smell, Low-Light Vision), Flame Projection, Immunity to Fire

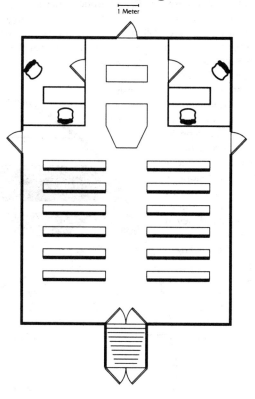

Policlub Meeting Hall

1 Meter

THE MEETING HALL

The meeting hall once belonged to the group Technocracy. The HNAL acquired it through a middleman several months ago. The HNAL voice-mail system is set up in an office to the right of the stage. (See the Policlub Meeting Hall archetype map, p. 32, **Sprawl Sites.**)

This room is as run-down as the rest of the building, with stained construction-plastic walls. A single desk, two chairs, and a small filing cabinet next to the door are the only furnishings in the room. The door is wired: opening it triggers a timer attached to an explosive charge in the filing cabinet. (This is the "surprise" mentioned earlier that the HNAL soldiers hope will soften up the runners.) Fifteen seconds after the door is opened, the charge detonates. It has a blast radius of 5 meters, and a damage code of 5M3. To more accurately determine the effects of the blast, the gamemaster should refer to the rules on explosive overpressure found on page 66 of the **Street Samurai Catalog.**

On the desk is a vid phone with the video subsystem disabled and a small personal computer. This is the HNAL's voice-mail system, described in more detail below.

The desk also holds a small appointment book with a synth-leather binding. Several pages are covered in scribbles that appear to be some kind of code. Actually, the scribbles are just that—meaningless scribbles. The appointment book is actually another "surprise" authored by the HNAL shaman. She has attuned the book as a spell lock for the spell Overstimulation, assuming that one of the runners will pocket the book for subsequent evaluation. Having the book on his or her person opens the runner up for the magical attack described in **Running the Gauntlet,** below.

Voice-Mail System

As described in **Hold the Phone**, the voice-mail system passes information between HNAL members. All voice messages are encrypted and stored on the machine's optical storage chip. A runner with Computer skill (or something close enough on the Skill Web) can try to decrypt the messages at a Target Number of 8. One success allows the runner to review all the messages on the chip.

Most of the messages consist of personal communications between members, reports on recruiting activities, and other mundane information. While these may be interesting curiosities, they are not important to the development of the adventure. One message is vitally important. It is time-stamped seven hours before the runners enter the building and appears in two personal mailboxes, Sheemahant's (labeled "Daniel") and Marta's ("Marta"). The message reads as follows:

"It's Wallace. The team is ready to go to the Klawock weapons lab and load out the last of the Red Masque. I know I'm behind schedule, but when we tested the integrity of the 'party suits', one showed a leak. We had to repair it before we could proceed. Better safe than dead, right? I'll give you a status update later."

The runners can locate Klawock on any public database, but they must work their local contacts to find out more about the lab itself. See **Legwork**, p. 44, for details on the weapons lab.

Gamemaster's Note: No matter how much damage the explosive charge does to the room, enough of the voice mail system will survive for the runners to acquire the optical chip.

RUNNING THE GAUNTLET

Unless a player character triggered the hell hound attack by scanning the building astrally when the runners arrived, the HNAL soldiers will be waiting for the team to leave the building (that is, anyone who survived the explosion). The sniper will target any easily identifiable mages or shamans (characters wearing cloaks with arcane symbols on them, visible fetishes, and so on) and try to take them down immediately. The remaining soldiers cut down anyone who wanders into the killing zone. The shaman will toss spells, or engage in astral combat with her surviving spellworms, whichever makes the most tactical sense.

If one of the runners pocketed the appointment book/spell lock from the office, the shaman will cast Overstimulation at him or her at once. As described on page 44 of the **Grimoire**, the spell lock makes the spell instantaneously permanent. (Nasty!) The HNAL shaman must have either visual or astral contact with the target.

AFTERMATH

If the team decrypts the optical chip in the voice-mail system, they receive enough background information to find out about the Klawock weapons lab. If they decide to visit Klawock and head off Wallace and his team, go to **Lab Work**, p. 29. If they hang out in Kemano for a few more hours, run **TerraFirst! at Last**, the next section.

DEBUGGING

Aside from getting greased in the ambush, the only way the team can get off track at this point is by ignoring the voice-mail system altogether, or failing to decrypt its contents. If they have managed to emerge from this encounter no wiser than they were, run **TerraFirst! at Last** next. This encounter gives them another chance to learn about the lab.

▼ ▼ ▼ ▼ ▼

TERRAFIRST! AT LAST

BEHIND THE SCENES

This encounter should take place after the runners start to make nuisances of themselves in Kemano. It can be a very nasty, extremely deadly little confrontation, but it will give the team another chance to find out about the Klawock lab.

Marta does not want the runners in Kemano asking dangerous questions and decides to eliminate them before they become a serious threat to her plans. She sends an assassination team after them. The assassins are TerraFirst! members, Cutup and Maumau (street samurai), and Smoke and Fire (hermetic mages). These four are intelligent and very skilled at their work, which is killing people. They will time their attack carefully to catch the runners' team at its most vulnerable, and will probably wait until the team is holed up for the night, when their defenses are at their weakest. Tough enough to give a good account of themselves in a stand-up fight, they prefer more subtle methods. If the team gives the TerraFirst! assassins even the slightest advantage, they will use it.

If the runners go to ground in a hotel, they will most likely put one of their members on astral patrol. Under normal circumstances, this would be a good idea. Unfortunately, this is just what Smoke and Fire hope for. The mages will move in astrally, and as soon as they spot the astral runner, they will pour all their physical spells into his astral body. This is bad news for the rest of the team, because, according to the **Grimoire**, when a physical spell strikes the astral body of a magician, the spell is grounded into that magician's physical body, wherever that might be. If the runner magician's body is in a hotel room with his buddies, fireballs and other nasty effects start bursting in the room, centered on the magician. Smoke and Fire will use Damaging Manipulation spells to affect their target without having to see him. (Any other spell requires visual or astral contact before the spell can be cast.)

Cutup

A chromed killing machine, James Darcy, alias Cutup, racked up an impressive list of credits as a freelance hit man before joining Marta and TerraFirst!. His specialty is "accidents." He prefers the indirect approach, though he executes direct tactics just as efficiently should they become necessary. He is cool under fire, and very logical at all times. He feels no loyalty to TerraFirst!, only to the money the group pays him. He will not throw his life away, but is professional enough to do what it takes to see a job through to its conclusion.

B	Q	S	C	I	W	E	M	R	Armor
5 (1)	5	4 (6)	4	5	5	.65	—	5 (7)	5/3

Dice Pools: Defense (Armed) 4, Defense (Unarmed) 4, Dodge 5
Skills: Armed Combat 4, Demolitions 4, Etiquette (Street) 5, Firearms 4 (Concentration: SMGs 6, Specialization: HK 227 SMG 8), Interrogation 3, Stealth 5, Unarmed Combat 4

Cyberware: Cyberlimbs (both arms) [w/Increased Strength (2), Smartgun Link (right), Retractable Spur (both)], Dermal Plating (1), Low-Light Eyes w/Flare Compensation and Thermographic, Wired Reflexes [1 (+1D6 Initiative)]
Gear: Armor Jacket (5/3), HK 227 [SMG, 20 (clip), 5M3, Built-in Smartgun Link, Silencer, and Gas-Vent Recoil Compensation (3)], Micro-transceiver, Three IPE Offensive Grenades (5S4)

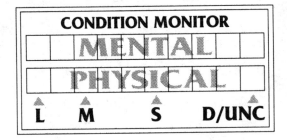

Maumau

Not quite as heavily chromed as Cutup, Maumau is definitely not off the rack. Amerindian by descent, the son of a Coyote shaman, Maumau inherited some of his father's creative, manic personality. He revels in combat, often taking what seem to be ludicrous risks for the sheer physical joy of the conflict. He is almost opposite in temperament to the cool, logical Cutup, making their close friendship somewhat surprising.

B	Q	S	C	I	W	E	M	R	Armor
4 (2)	6 (7)	4 (5)	5	4	4	.3	—	5 (7)	4/3

Dice Pools: Defense (Armed) 5, Defense (Unarmed) 6, Dodge 6 (7)
Skills: Armed Combat 5, Etiquette (Street) 4, Firearms 6 (Concentration: Pistols 8), Stealth 4, Unarmed Combat 6
Cyberware: Dermal Plating (2), Low-Light Eyes w/Flare Compensation and Thermographic, Muscle Replacement (1), Retractable Razors (both hands), Smartgun Link, Wired Reflexes [1 (+1D6 Initiative)]
Gear: Ares Predator II [Heavy Pistol, 15 (clip), 6M2, w/Silencer and Built-in Smartgun Link], Micro-transceiver, Vest with Plates (4/3)

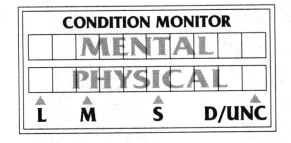

Smoke and Fire

Smoke and Fire are identical twin sisters (really Brandi and Candi Maythorpe), about 25 years old, blonde, and gorgeous. While they may look—and sometimes act—like harmless ex-cheerleaders, they are actually cold-blooded, magically adept killers. Unlike their teammates, Smoke and Fire are emotional disciples of Marta and true believers in the TerraFirst! cause. This devotion makes them much more likely to sacrifice their lives for the success of the mission. Both are Grade 3 Initiates and use Latin incantations as their Centering skill. Their magical concentration is fire magic (pyromancy). The sisters are virtually inseparable, and their street names come from the old adage, "Where there's smoke, there's fire." If one sister is killed, the other will fight to her own death to avenge her sister.

B	Q	S	C	I	W	E	M	R	Armor
3	4	3	3	6	5	6	5	5	5/3

Dice Pools: Astral (as Skill), Astral Dodge 6, Astral Magic 5 (11), Astral Special 3, Defense (Armed) 2, Defense (Unarmed) 1, Dodge 4, Magic 5 (11)

Skills: Armed Combat 2, Conjuring 6, Etiquette (Street) 2, Firearms 3, Magical Theory 6, Sorcery 5, Stealth 3, Unarmed Combat 1

Gear: Ares Viper [Heavy Pistol, 30 (clip), 2M3, w/Laser Sight], Armor Jacket (5/3), Knife (Weapon Focus 2), Micro-transceiver, Wrist Bracelet (Power Focus 6)

Spells: Fire Bolt 2, Fire Cloud 3, Fire Dart 4, Fire Missile 4, Fireball 4, Flame Bomb 5, Ignite 4, Medium Body Decrease 4

If the runners interrogate one of the assassins, they can learn the information given in **Legwork** for the following topics: the HNAL, Daniel Sheemahant, Marta, the Kemano substation raid, and TerraFirst!. None of the assassins know anything about Marta's overall plans, though all four have overheard her talking about some lab in Klawock. Of course, extracting this kind of information from a team of hardened assassins will not be easy.

The runners can go to **Lab Work**, the next section, if they decide to visit Klawock, or to **Sunday Papers**, p. 33, if they once again fail to come up with any information.

DEBUGGING

The possibility exists that the team will geek the assassins and so remain ignorant of Klawock. Two options are still open. One is to let the runners cool their heels in Kemano, running **Sunday Papers** to get them back into the action. This option skips their visit to the Klawock weapons lab.

The second option is a little trickier to pull off. One of the attackers keeps a diary on a pocket micro-recorder that chronicles overheard conversations and other sensitive information. Klawock and a weapons lab are mentioned several times; these clues should point the runners in the right direction.

TELL IT TO THEM STRAIGHT

So this is Prince of Wales Island. A rocky hell lashed by vicious winds and freezing squalls straight off the frigid Gulf of Alaska. The thick, dark forests seem filled with brooding, implacable hostility against insignificant creatures like yourself. According to the public databanks, though, the island wasn't always like this. Several towns, including Craig, Hydaburg, and Point Baker used to thrive here. There's nothing much left of them now, and the island is virtually deserted. Klawock itself was once a prosperous fishing community on the island's west coast, but it too is now uninhabited. The deserted buildings here seem to have held up a little better against the elements than those elsewhere on Prince of Wales. Probably because they were built from prestressed ferroconcrete rather than wood or other lighter, native building materials. Klawock is surrounded by the decrepit remains of a high fence that reminds you of nothing so much as a military base…or a concentration camp.

Klawock Base

N
W   E
S

= 1.5 METERS

BEHIND THE SCENES

No regular transportation runs to Prince of Wales Island, and so the runners must find their own way across. A rotorcraft is their best bet because the island offers few places where a winged plane (other than a VTOL of some kind) can set down safely.

In the early years of the 21st century, Klawock was held as a military base, hence the fence and blockhouse-like buildings. The entrance to the underground lab the runners are looking for is in a building near the center of the base.

The area of the deserted base has a magical Background Count of 2 (see **The Grimoire**, p. 63). Anyone assensing the area can tell that this is an unhealthy place to be, the site of evil doings some time in the past. (The Background Count is too low to give any idea of just what kind of evil was perpetrated. An overall negative feeling, a "spiritual blight," just hangs about the region.)

KLAWOCK BASE

What is left of a high fence surrounds the entire base. Most of the support posts remain, but very little of the fence itself has survived the test of time. Examination of any one of the supports will reveal the remnants of insulators, revealing that the fence used to be electrified.

All the buildings are ferroconcrete blockhouse structures that have been efficiently emptied. Buildings that might interest the players' characters are described below.

KLAWOCK BASE MAP KEY

Main Gate (1)
The base's heavy gate is still shut and locked—which is amusing, because the section of fence just to the right of the gatehouse is completely gone.

Base Office (2)
This building is empty, but recognizable for what it was.

Generator Building (3)
This building contains the high-power, high-efficiency petrochem-fueled generator used to provide power to the entire base. The machinery is still in place, but rusted into inoperability long ago.

Access Building (4)
Virtually indistinguishable from the other buildings, this small structure near the center of the base houses the access elevator for the underground weapons lab. The TerraFirst! team has set up a high-efficiency generator in this building to run the elevator. When the runners arrive at the building, the elevator is at the bottom of the shaft at lab level, about 30 meters below ground. It responds to the call button, however, and arrives at ground level in 45 seconds.

When it arrives, the elevator contains two HNAL soldiers, members of the team Wallace Blackwood brought to remove the last of the bioweapons from the lab. They were waiting in the elevator for their colleagues and were trapped inside when the doors suddenly shut. They have no communications gear, and so cannot warn the rest of the team that someone else is on the base. The soldiers know that no one else should be in Klawock, and will come out of the elevator shooting.

The elevator has only two buttons, up and down. Pressing the down button sends the elevator to the lab level.

Blackwood did not expect trouble, but as a matter of course set up a Force 2 ward across the elevator shaft. He also conjured a Force 3 hearth spirit to guard against other spellcasters. (See **The Grimoire**, p. 69, for information about wards.) Blackwood immediately becomes aware of anyone trying to break through his wards and sets up an ambush outside the elevator at lab level.

THE LAB

The underground lab's only illumination comes from the battery-powered lights placed at intervals by Blackwood's team. The lighting is far from bright, giving a +1 penalty to all target numbers for ranged combat. (Low-light or thermographic vision eliminates this penalty.)

In its heyday, the lab was an extensive complex. When the U.S. military pulled out, however, they planted FAE (fuel-air explosive) bombs throughout the place to destroy it. Some of these bombs were duds, and a small area of the lab survived. The rubble shown on the map cannot be cleared by any means. The sections of the lab beyond the rubble were buried when the charges collapsed the ceilings.

Blackwood's fears to the contrary, the air in the lab complex is clean. The runners have no way of knowing this, of course, so play on their fears that invisible death lurks in every breath they take. The air is musty and has a slight chemical taste, a result of minuscule leaks from the FAE explosive devices that failed to detonate. The gas leak is harmless, too diluted to cause a fire or explosion hazard. (As discussed below, the FAE bomb itself is another story.)

Walls, ceilings, and floors are reinforced concrete (Barrier Rating 32), and all doors are reinforced impact plastic (Barrier Rating 20).

UNDERGROUND LAB MAP KEY

Elevator (1)

The elevator runs from the ground level to the lab level.

Corridor (2)

A two-meter long metal object that looks like a blunt bullet is bolted to the floor in the middle of the corridor. This is one of the FAE (fuel-air explosive) bombs that the U.S. military planted to destroy the complex. This bomb did not detonate.

An FAE bomb is basically a large pressurized tank of highly explosive gas and several detonating "squibs." When the bomb is triggered, valves open to release the gas into the atmosphere. Several seconds later, the squibs fire, detonating the gas-air mixture. The bomb's metal skin is fairly thin, with a Barrier Rating of 5 against gunfire. Indiscriminate gunplay may puncture the bomb and release explosive gas into the air.

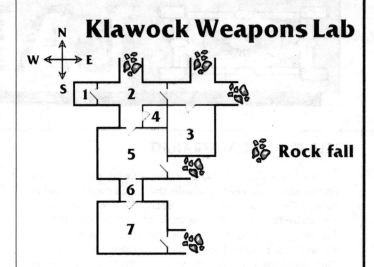

The two teams meeting in the underground lab are luckier than they know. The gas in the bomb degraded over the years and is nowhere near as explosive as it was originally. If the gas is released, any open flames will burn twice as hot and twice as large as normal, doing twice their normal damage. Any small explosive event, such as a gunshot or an appropriate (Damaging Manipulations) magic spell may trigger a limited detonation of the gas. Each time a gun is fired in the gas-contaminated air, roll 2D6. A result of 2 means that the gas around the gun has ignited, creating a limited-area fireball. This fireball has a radius of one meter (it will probably affect only the gunman himself) and a damage code of 3M3. It is impossible for a chance shot to detonate the entire FAE bomb. (Neither the runners nor the HNAL troops know this, however, which should put a damper on uncontrolled firefights.)

Computer Room (3)

This room contains four terminals connected to a central minicomputer. No power is available for the machines, but creative runners might be able to hook up a portable power supply. If the team's decker fires up the system and attempts to deck into it, he will discover only that the archaic microprocessor system is long dead.

A much easier way to find out what is stored on the system is to simply open up the machine and remove the computer's long-term memory, a magnetic-media hard drive. Recognizing the appropriate component requires a single success on a Computer Skill Test against a Target Number of 5. A Computer B/R (4) Test is required to jury-rig the hard drive so it will work and to access it with an appropriate piece of modern computer technology. No IC protects the drive itself, so reviewing the contents poses no risk. (See the **Lab Computer System** for the contents of the drive.)

Locker Room (4)

Twenty metal lockers line the walls of this room. Private lockers for the scientists who worked in the complex, most are empty. Their owners cleaned them out before they left. Four still contain chemsuits.

Chemistry Lab (5)

This lab developed the non-toxic components of the inoculant, or vaccine, for the Red Masque viral agent (see **Lab Computer System**). The room contains a number of long workbenches and two refrigerators. No expensive or scientifically complex equipment remains. An administrative screw-up ("I thought Jim was supposed to handle that!"), left ten vials, each containing one dose of the Red Masque inoculant and labeled as such, in one of the refrigerators. The fridges are not cold any more, of course, but the inoculant is still active (though the runners may not know that). The inoculant must be injected to take effect (much like a measles shot).

Air Lock (6)

This short, narrow corridor's doors are fitted with air-tight rubber gaskets. An electronic interlock used to control the doors: while one door was open, the other was locked. Without power, both doors can be open at the same time. The door into the **Bioengineering Lab (7)** is marked with the biohazard trefoil.

Bioengineering Lab (7)

The layout here is similar to the chemistry lab, with lab tables and refrigerators. A map showing the border between the Tsimshian Nation and the Athabascan Council is stuck to the side of one of the refrigerators. A red circle labeled "Test Zone" marks an area near the town of Telegraph Creek on the Stikine River. As in the chemistry lab, all of the wiz tech toys are gone. The same administrative screw-up is responsible for one of these fridges still containing the Red Masque virus. When the runners arrive at the lab, Blackwood's team is in this area loading four containers of Red Masque virus into an armored, padded, suitcase-sized case. If the runners alert Blackwood to their presence by messing with the wards he set, or if he becomes aware that something is going on elsewhere in the lab, he and his team quickly finish packing the virus and prepare to deal with the intruders. The Red Masque is in metal cylinders about 20 cm long and 6 cm in diameter, marked in red with the biohazard trefoil.

BLACKWOOD'S TEAM

Information on Wallace Blackwood appears in **Cast of Shadows**, p. 46. If encountered here, he is wearing a chemsuit identical to those worn by the rest of his team. This makes it difficult, if not impossible, for the runners to decide who is in command. Blackwood is accompanied by nine HNAL soldiers (in addition to the two in the elevator). He is also served by a hearth spirit of Force 3, and has set a ward to block the elevator shaft.

One of the soldiers carries an armored suitcase containing four metal containers of Red Masque virus. If the runners mess with these containers—clearly marked with the biohazard symbol—and release the contents, anyone within 20 feet of the broken container breathing ambient, unfiltered air will be infected by Red Masque.

HNAL Soldiers (Nine)

These soldiers count among the "true believers" of the HNAL and serve as the organization's main shock troops. Most have at least some military training, and all are skilled at small-unit tactics. Like well-motivated soldiers everywhere, they will risk or even sacrifice their lives to save their colleagues, but they will not throw their lives away in foolish heroics. If forced into a tactically untenable situation—i.e., if they are losing big time and know it—they will surrender rather than fight to the death.

B	Q	S	C	I	W	E	M	R	Armor
4	3	4	3	3	6	—	3		3/0

Dice Pools: Defense (Armed) 5, Defense (Unarmed) 3, Dodge 3

Skills: Armed Combat 5, Etiquette (Street) 3, Etiquette (Tribal) 4, Firearms 5, Military Theory 2, Stealth 2, Throwing Weapons 2, Unarmed Combat 3

Gear: Chemsuit over Armor Clothing (3/0), Knife (2L1), Scorpion Machine Pistol [Light Pistol, 35 (clip), 3M2 APDS, w/Laser Sight]

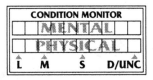
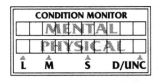
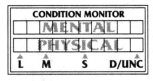
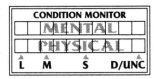
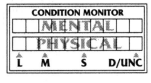
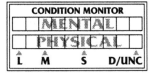
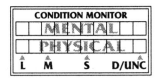

THE LAB COMPUTER SYSTEM

The minicomputer in the **Computer Room (3)** contains records describing the various nasties the lab created for the U.S. military. The records on the computer's hard drive are encrypted, but the algorithm is fairly simple. After all, the security system is several decades out of date, and the military expected the computer's IC to handle most intruders.

The lab created three highly unpleasant nerve gases they named Green Ring 1, 2, and 3. The chemical formulae does not appear on these chips; these records reference other records, stored on another computer, presumably somewhere in the collapsed areas of the complex. In any case, the records show that the Green Ring projects were canceled some three years before the lab was closed down.

At the time the lab was decommissioned (read "evacuated and destroyed"), only one project was still active, something called Project Red Masque. According to the computer, Red Masque is a viral agent designed to be delivered in an aerosol suspension. The Red Masque virus attacks the central nervous system of humans and metahumans, causing a progressive loss of mental functions and eventual death. The time course for the viral infection is several days. The military considered this time

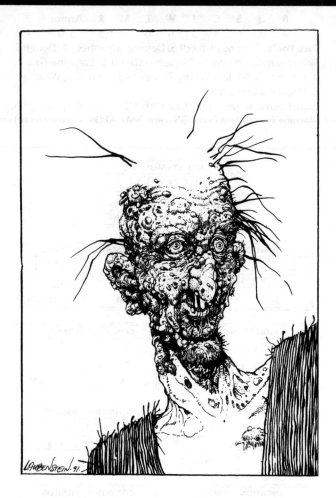

frame desirable because even one infected victim could tie up medical resources for some time, causing more disruption than would instant death. The virus cannot be passed on by an infected victim; as soon as the virus enters the bloodstream, it undergoes a chemical change that makes it non-contagious. The symptoms of Red Masque include red blotches on the skin, excessive nasal mucous (i.e., a bad runny nose), hair loss, disorientation, loss of concentration, and eventual delirium and death. In game terms, a victim infected by Red Masque loses one point each of Body, Intelligence, and Willpower every 24 hours. When any of these attributes reaches zero, the victim dies. The effects of Red Masque can be countered by magic. To calculate resistance and the effects of Prophylaxis spells, treat Red Masque as a type S pathogen.

Red Masque also affects large mammals, any warm-blooded creature with a body mass of over 40 kg (about 90 lbs). The time course is much faster for animals. They usually die within 12 hours of infection.

Red Masque is an almost perfect war virus. Infection from the original aerosol vector is almost 100 percent, and without magical intervention, over 90 percent lethal. The virus is susceptible to the ultraviolet light of sunlight. Within 24 hours of its release, the living virus remains only within the bodies of infected victims (and they are not infectious, as discussed above). This would allow an attacker to hit a city with Red Masque, wait a day, then enter the area at no personal risk.

The computer records also contain the chemical formula for a vaccine, or inoculation, against Red Masque. One dose protects a human or metahuman against Red Masque for 72 hours. If the vaccine is injected into a human or metahuman suffering from Red Masque, the chemical kills the virus in the victim's body and reverses the symptoms of the disease. The victim regains one point each of Body, Intelligence, and Willpower every 48 hours until all attributes are back to their normal levels. An individual cured by this vaccine can be reinfected by Red Masque.

The vaccine is difficult and expensive to produce. It can only be formulated in a well-equipped chemistry lab by a character with Physical Sciences skill (Concentration: Chemistry). The raw materials for one dose cost 450¥. A chemist can concoct one batch comprising a number of doses equal to his Intelligence. Creating a batch takes 10 hours, and has a Target Number of 6. The chemist needs only one success in order for the batch to be successful, but without at least one success, the procedure has failed. He can try again, but the procedure will take another 10 hours. If the chemist rolls all 1s, he has hosed it big time and has destroyed the raw materials. Time to start again from scratch.

The minicomputer does not give details for how to bioengineer the Red Masque virus. Enough information is provided, however, that a skilled bioengineer could "reverse engineer" the virus. The level of skill necessary is far beyond what any runner will possess. (In other words, forget about trying it yourself, chummer.) Many organizations in the runners' world would just love to get their hands on the information in the lab. Unscrupulous runners might decide to sell the data on the open market. This will net them a profit on the order of 10,000¥, but selling it is a bad idea. For example, if they sold the data to MCT, it is entirely likely that the megacorp would incorporate Red Masque into its security systems. Sell the data, and you might just end up with a face-full of Red Masque yourself on a future run. Bad karma, man.

AFTERMATH

Blackwood will fight to the death, but the HNAL soldiers are less fanatical, making it quite likely that the runners will keep someone alive for interrogation. Blackwood knows only that Marta and Sheemahant have big plans for the Red Masque virus. He has no details. The soldiers have even less information, but can venture an informed guess about what is going down. Any surviving team member can tell the runners that the HNAL/TerraFirst! group has a base over the border in the Athabascan Council lands near a place called Telegraph Creek on the Stikine River. The base is the drop-off for the last of the virus liberated from the lab. If the runners geek everyone, then the first body they search has a scrawled note describing this location.

If the runners decide to check out the base, go to **Dead Zone**, p. 34, giving them the information on the "Dead Zone" from **Sunday Papers** first. If they miss this piece of information, go to **Sunday Papers** to get them back on track.

DEBUGGING

Unless they die, the runners should find it difficult to get off track here. Even if they fail to pick up the information on the HNAL/TerraFirst! base, **Sunday Papers** gives them a chance to get back with the program.

It is possible that team members might come down with the Red Masque viral disease. If that happens, let them suffer the symptoms for a while, then make pointed hints about getting magical help to shake the bug.

BEHIND THE SCENES

This scene is to be used only if the team has gotten hopelessly off track: if they lost Blackwood, missed the information on the HNAL/TerraFirst! base near Telegraph Creek, or are otherwise foundering. This scene may also be used if the entire team managed to get themselves geeked. A second team, possibly friends or relatives of the first group, can pick up from here.

Several days after the events in **TerraFirst! at Last** and **Lab Work**, the team hears an unusual item on the news media: According to officially substantiated reports, a strange plague has hit just over the border in Athabascan Council territory. This unidentified plague appears to have killed all mammalian life in a three-kilometer radius. This area, dubbed the "Dead Zone" by the media, lies just south of the town of Telegraph Creek on the Stikine River. The media is full of wild speculation about what could have caused this plague. The runners should guess that it is related to bioweapons, and worth checking out.

If the runners have learned that the HNAL has a base in the Stikine region, give them the Dead Zone information from the media anyway.

The runners must cross the border into the Athabascan Council and get to the Stikine region on their own.

DEBUGGING

If the runners fail to pick up on the connection between the Dead Zone and bioweapons, or opt not to follow up on it, forget the whole adventure: as shadowrunners they are not worth the paper they are printed on. Suggest that the team take up crochet or Scrabble.

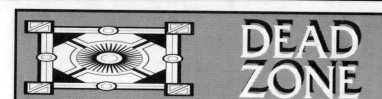

DEAD ZONE

TELL IT TO THEM STRAIGHT

The Stikine River area will never make it as a resort destination. It's a frigid region of rolling foothills and snow-covered tundra. You remember reading that it wasn't always like this, that weather patterns have changed drastically since the Awakening and nobody knows why. That's ancient history, though. You've got to deal with the world as it is, not as it was. The wind cuts through you as you approach the boundaries of what the media calls the Dead Zone.

Keen eyes, both meat and electronic, scan the horizon. There's something out there. Six small black dots are coming across the snow. The wind carries the angry whining of small engines revved up high.

BEHIND THE SCENES

The six approaching dots are members of a local thrill gang that calls itself the Polar Bears. Mounted on snowmobiles, like all thrill gangs they make trouble for anybody unfortunate enough to cross their path, just as a matter of course.

This group of thrill-gangers is different, however. They have been infected by the Red Masque virus. The Polar Bears show the physical symptoms of the viral agent; red, blotchy skin, profuse nasal discharge, and severe hair loss. If the team viewed the computer records in the Klawock lab, they will quickly recognize these symptoms for what they are.

The viral infection has made the Polar Bears more violent than normal. Today, they will fight to the death, willingly getting themselves geeked and doing their best to take an honor guard with them. If the team can keep at least one (or more) ganger alive long enough to interrogate him, they can learn the following information.

•Five days ago, the "Dead Zone" was normal. Three days ago, when the gang last passed through the region, all the mammals were dead.

•The Polar Bears have been feeling worse than drek for the last three days.

•A really tough group has a temporary base about 15 klicks north of the Dead Zone. The Polar Bears went up to work them over, but ended up barely escaping, and with severe casualties. (This camp is, of course, the HNAL/TerraFirst! base.)

Though the team may not know this—and might not believe it even if they scanned the entire Red Masque file from the Klawock lab—the Dead Zone is now safe. Sunlight killed the virus. The Polar Bears were unlucky enough to wander into Marta's field test while the virus was still active. Let the runners take whatever (unnecessary) precautions they need to make them feel safe.

Polar Bear Ganger (Six)

Typical north-country thrill-gangers, the Polar Bears consider anyone they meet to be "raw meat," something to chew up just for the fun of it.

(The attributes in parentheses are the reduced values resulting from Red Masque infection.)

B	Q	S	C	I	W	E	M	R	Armor
4	4	5(2)	3	4(1)	4(1)	6	—	4(2)	3/0

Dice Pools: Defense (Armed) 5, Defense (Unarmed) 5, Dodge 4
Skills: Armed Combat 5, Etiquette (Street) 4, Firearms 5, Snowmobile 3, Unarmed Combat 5
Gear: Armor Clothing (3/0), Colt America L36 [Light Pistol, 9 (clip), 3M2], Knife (1L1)

CONDITION MONITOR
MENTAL
PHYSICAL
L M S D/UNC

CONDITION MONITOR
MENTAL
PHYSICAL
L M S D/UNC

CONDITION MONITOR
MENTAL
PHYSICAL
L M S D/UNC

CONDITION MONITOR
MENTAL
PHYSICAL
L M S D/UNC

CONDITION MONITOR
MENTAL
PHYSICAL
L M S D/UNC

CONDITION MONITOR
MENTAL
PHYSICAL
L M S D/UNC

In addition to a pistol, three of the Polar Bears carry Remington 750 hunting rifles [5 (magazine), 5S2]. These weapons cannot be fired while the snowmobiles are in motion, however.

Use the following statistics for the snowmobiles: Handling 3, Speed 40/90, Body 1, Armor 0, Signature 4, Pilot 0.

When the team is ready to investigate the HNAL camp, go to **A Little Too Late**, the next section.

DEBUGGING

If the team geeks all the gangers, there is still a chance they will find out about the HNAL base. One of the gangers considered himself something of a writer, and kept a handwritten journal of his life. In rather overblown—and badly misspelled—prose, this journal describes the abortive raid against an armed camp on the Stikine River some 10 kilometers north of the Dead Zone.

The Polar Bears should serve as a nuisance encounter and a source of information, not a donnybrook to kill the team off. If the team starts going down, fudge the dice rolls a little to keep them alive and in reasonably good shape. As always, the gamemaster must conceal the fact that he is helping the runners out. Make it look natural: a wounded ganger loses control of his snowmobile and plows into two of his fellows, a wild shot detonates a fuel tank, geeking several gangers at once, and so on.

A LITTLE TOO LATE

TELL IT TO THEM STRAIGHT

Ten kilometers north of the Dead Zone along the Stikine River. Not the most complete set of directions. But, as it turns out, they're good enough. You see the camp while you're still a klick or so off. It's a group of perhaps half-a-dozen small, prefab buildings, set on the snowy ground near the river. From this distance, it looks like nothing's moving.

If a team member assenses the area astrally, read the following.

Your breathing and heartbeat settle to a calm basal rate. You feel a familiar tingle of excitement as your astral being slips out of your body. Invisibly, intangibly, you float toward the camp.

Your original assessment was right, you realize. The camp is deserted. From the piles of garbage and the disposable equipment left behind, you know it was occupied very recently. But the inhabitants have obviously pulled out.

If the team explores the camp physically, read the following.

Your original assessment was right. The camp is deserted. From the piles of garbage and the disposable equipment left behind, you know it was occupied very recently. But the inhabitants have obviously pulled out.

BEHIND THE SCENES

The HNAL/TerraFirst! team actually left the camp only 24 hours or so before the runners arrived. If the runners trashed Blackwood and his group at Klawock, Marta will have learned about it through her spirit contacts and sounded the alarm. If the runners did not visit Klawock, Blackwood and his boys arrived at the camp 24 hours ago, and everyone promptly headed out to put the next part of the plan into motion.

THE CAMP

"Camp" is almost too grand a word for this site, because it consists of nothing more than five 4 x 6 meter prefabricated buildings made from thin construction plastic (Barrier Rating 2).

The "operations shack" is in the center of the camp. This is where Marta and Sheemahant held briefings and trained their soldiers. A portable computer system was set up here, but they took it with them when they left. Any runner entering the hut should make a Perception (8) Test; if the runner is actively searching the hut, the Target Number drops to 4.

If a runner achieves even one success, read him the following.

They cleaned this place out pretty well. Disgusted at your lack of success at finding even the smallest clue as to what's going on, you kick at the dirt floor as you head for the door. Then you catch a glimpse of something on the floor glinting in the light. Excited now, you kneel to get a better view of your find. It's an optical chip.

The information on the chip is described below. Another valuable clue awaits discovery in the hut, but again, the player characters must be actively searching and make a successful Perception (9) Test.

The hut's door frame fits badly, and a short but sharp edge sticks out. A tiny scrap of fabric is caught on the projection, and a minuscule amount of blood stains the fabric. Both fabric and blood are Marta's; she brushed the door frame as she was leaving and did not even feel the tiny wound. The blood is sufficient to allow a skilled magician to track Marta astrally. Of course, the mage will not know just who is being tracked. One of the soldiers, or even an uninvited guest, such as a Polar Bear thrill-ganger, may have nicked himself on the door frame. The clue could be worthless. (Which it is not.) Astral tracking will show that Marta is currently on an island just inside Douglas Channel, the body of water on whose coast lies Kitimat, the capital city of Tsimshian. If the team has some way of comparing this astrally acquired location to a map, they find that Marta is currently on the southern tip of Hawkesbury Island.

THE CHIP

When the HNAL/TerraFirst! force abandoned their camp, they loaded out all their training equipment and material. When they packed the computer, however, somebody carelessly dropped an optical storage chip. The information on the chip is not encrypted, so anyone with a computer system or cyberdeck can read its contents.

The chip contains the complete deck plans of a medium-sized ship identified only as the "TMV Queen of the North." The plans are reproduced in **Over the Bounding Main**, p. 38. A quick scan of the public databases will tell the runners that the Tsimshian Motor Vessel *Queen of the North* is one of the reconditioned ferries running the Inside Passage route from Port Hardy in Salish-Shidhe to Kitimat. The schedule tells the runners that the vessel left Port Hardy at almost the same moment they first viewed the ship's deck plans, and is due to arrive in Kitimat 12 hours later. (The team now has a little deadline pressure.)

A note attached to the file reads "F3-10.32.01/28.41.90." Any character skilled in Navigation (a possible Special Skill), Motorboat, or Sailboat will immediately recognize this as a reference to a specific location on a nautical chart. If none of the runners has the appropriate skill to recognize the information, the team should hit the databases again to try to identify the annotation. Searching when you have no idea what it is you are looking for is no picnic, and requires a Computer (6) Test. One success identifies the annotation as a nautical chart reference.

Once the runners know the reference is to a nautical chart, they must get the appropriate chart and find the location. This is a simple task, but the team must make the effort to accomplish it. If they give it a shot, they find that chart reference F3-10.32.01/28.41.90 is a small patch of water in the Douglas Channel between Hawkesbury Island and Hartley Bay on the mainland. This location lies approximately 67 klicks southwest of Kitimat on the TMV *Queen of the North*'s approach course to the capital. A quick calculation later, and the runners can estimate that the ferry will reach this particular chunk of ocean about 10 hours after the team first viewed the contents of the chip. Even someone who is not a rocket scientist will figure out that something significant is going to happen when the *Queen of the North* reaches that location.

Go to **Over the Bounding Main**, p. 37.

DEBUGGING

This encounter sets up the final, climactic meeting aboard the TMV *Queen of the North* in Douglas Channel. The runners must learn where they need to go next in this encounter. The target numbers provided above for the various skill tests should show the gamemaster how much the runners should sweat to get the paydata, not become a way to skunk them. If the players' dice are ice cold, the gamemaster may want to modify the results somehow so the team learns the information they need to complete the task Farseer set. The gamemaster should also make the team sweat, however. Roll a ludicrous number of dice, stare at them, and shake your head while making "tsk-tsk" noises. At this point, good players will no doubt deluge you with new tactics for getting the information and reasons why those tactics should succeed. If the players (not their characters) show some creativity, give them the information without revealing that it is a gift. If you need to, draw on the background the players have developed for their characters. ("Jill, you said your character Scalpel grew up in a fishing village on the Pacific Coast? Scalpel remembers, out of the blue, the maritime chart mounted on the wall of her dad's office, marked with the locations of the best fishing grounds," and so on.)

On the other hand, if the players seem uninterested in the ultimate fate of the Tsimshian region, and undisturbed by the nastiness of the quarry they are chasing, let the dice rule. If they get skunked, they get skunked. As described in **Picking Up the Pieces**, the runner team has some backup working for them that they know nothing about.

Some players may want to turn the whole mess over to the Tsimshian authorities and let them handle things. This is a bad idea for at least two reasons. First of all, what kind of credibility would a bunch of chromed shadowrunners, reeking of cordite, have with the Tsimshian government? Right you are, chummer: exactly none. The Tsimshian authorities would probably just lock the team up and forget about them. Secondly, Tsimshian is a bureaucracy, which means it would probably take several precious hours just to get access to someone with enough clout to accomplish anything. Even then, said person with clout would probably use it against the runners. No, going to the authorities is not a good move.

Looks like the team will be forced into a combat situation.

·MIKE NIELSEN 91·

OVER THE BOUNDING MAIN

TELL IT TO THEM STRAIGHT

The TMV *Queen of the North* is a sleek, swept-bow craft, with a single stack and two oversized instrument masts bristling with old-tech radar gear. Even to your untrained eyes, the design looks archaic, quite different from the other deep-sea vessels that ply the oceans, but it does have a peculiar charm. You can see that the entire bow section swings up to give access to the car deck, a design similar to certain military transport aircraft like the Stratolifter III. The *Queen of the North* sports the same paint job it had when it was a BC Ferries Corporation vessel at the end of the last century: mainly white, trimmed with red and blue. The white has become a putrid yellow, however, and rust stains spread over much of the ship's hull.

BEHIND THE SCENES

The first problem for the team is to intercept the TMV *Queen of the North*. By the time they reach the coast, the ship has set sail. They can "acquire" a boat of some kind and approach the ship by sea, or try to lay their hands on an aircraft and come after it from above. As the deck plans show, however, nothing but the smallest VTOL or rotorcraft could land onboard—assuming that the HNAL/TerraFirst! soldiers quietly accept such an attempt (which is unlikely). The ship is also not equipped to have passengers board from another seagoing vessel. The team is entirely on its own when it comes to getting aboard the ferry. (The gamemaster should not sweat this difficulty. If the players' characters are any kind of shadowrunners, they will already have half a dozen plans for overcoming this problem.)

QUEEN OF THE NORTH

The TMV *Queen of the North* is a sleek ocean-going vessel with a keel length of approximately 125 meters, a beam of about 19.4 meters, and a total displacement of 8,890 tons (yes, it is big). Its hull and decks are reinforced steel, with a Barrier Rating of 24, and all interior bulkheads and doors are thick steel, with a Barrier Rating of 12. This tough vessel has the following statistics:

Handling	Speed	B/A	Sig	APilot
3	30/35	24/0	1	2

When it set sail from Port Hardy, the *Queen* had a crew of 30; 6 engine crew, 6 bridge crew, and 18 other miscellaneous crew including purser, stewards, and so on. It also carried 55 passengers. Unfortunately for everyone else aboard, 20 of those passengers were actually HNAL soldiers (use the stats provided in **Lab Work**, but without the chemsuits and with armored jackets (5/3) in place of armored clothing). Exactly one hour after the *Queen of the North* set sail, the HNAL troops pulled out their weapons and took over the ship, geeking everyone else aboard. Four troops now man the engine spaces, tending the

diesels, and four are on the bridge, with the other twelve scattered around on deck making modifications necessary to the next step of Marta's plan. The soldiers on the bridge are familiar enough with communications protocol between the ferry and the ports to simulate appropriate status reports, and so nobody suspects that anything untoward has happened.

The *Queen* is scheduled to meet up with Marta, Sheemahant, and their men in Douglas Channel, between Hawkesbury Island and Hartley Bay on the mainland. When it reaches this point it will stop. The plan is to load the Red Masque aboard, abandon the vessel, and send it into Kitimat harbor on autopilot.

If the team tries to board the *Queen of the North* before this rendezvous takes place, the HNAL soldiers will fight to the death to repulse the attack. In addition to personal weapons, the troops have two man-portable missile launcher tubes, each supplied with four anti-vehicular missiles, or AVMs (Intelligence 4, Ammo 4, Damage 12D8/6D4). Assume that four HNAL soldiers are competent with these weapons (Gunnery 4).

If the team survives the boarding party, they can take control of the *Queen of the North*. Their next move is up to them. They can continue on course and hope to ambush Marta and crew. They can reverse course and return to Port Hardy, or they can head off on a cruise if that option strikes their fancy. Taking the ship will prevent Marta from following through on her plan to strike at Kitimat, but she will be left on the loose, and the runners will have only postponed the inevitable. The same is true if the runners simply sink the *Queen of the North*.

An assault on a ferry is a perfect opportunity for the runners to use all those wizzer heavy weapons that are just inappropriate for day-to-day use on the city streets. The gamemaster could suggest that they visit an armorer and load up before they go after the *Queen of the North*.

MARTA AND CREW

The group scheduled to meet with the ferry comprises Marta, Sheemahant, Wallace Blackwood (if he survived the **Lab Work** encounter), and 15 HNAL soldiers. They have two vessels.

GMC Riverine

Handling	Speed	B/A	Sig	APilot
3	30/90	4/2	3	2

Seating: 2 bucket seats
Mounts: Port and starboard hardpoints mounting an HMG and assault cannon, respectively, with 5 clips of ammo for each

Samuvani Chriscraft Otter

Handling	Speed	B/A	Sig	APilot
4	15/45	2/0	3	2

Seating: 2 bucket seats plus 4 folding bench seats
Mounts: 2 firmpoints packing the equivalent of an AK-97 (50 rounds) each

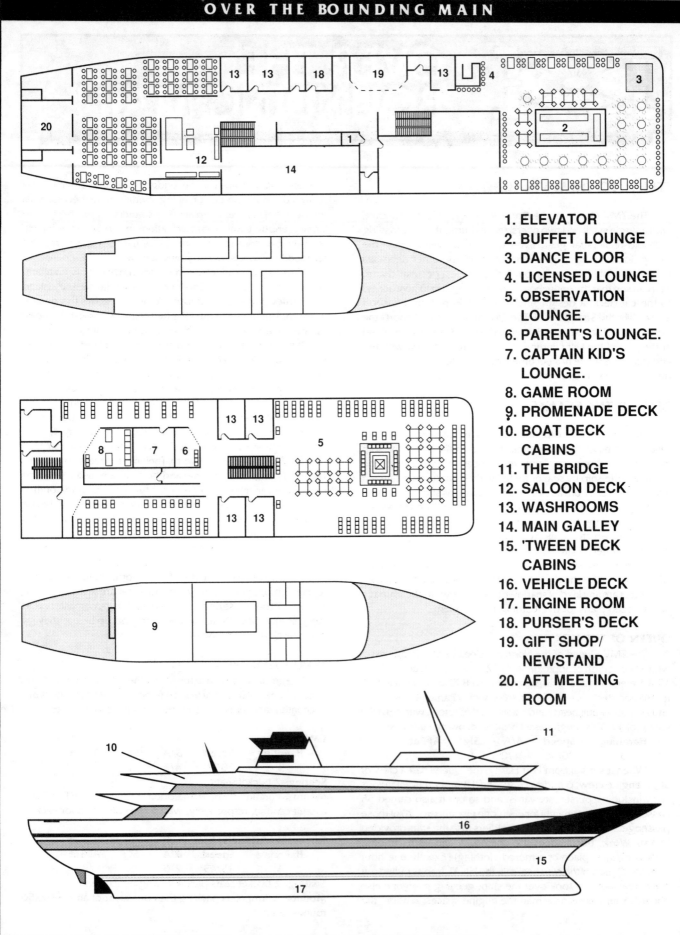

1. **ELEVATOR**
2. **BUFFET LOUNGE**
3. **DANCE FLOOR**
4. **LICENSED LOUNGE**
5. **OBSERVATION LOUNGE.**
6. **PARENT'S LOUNGE.**
7. **CAPTAIN KID'S LOUNGE.**
8. **GAME ROOM**
9. **PROMENADE DECK**
10. **BOAT DECK CABINS**
11. **THE BRIDGE**
12. **SALOON DECK**
13. **WASHROOMS**
14. **MAIN GALLEY**
15. **'TWEEN DECK CABINS**
16. **VEHICLE DECK**
17. **ENGINE ROOM**
18. **PURSER'S DECK**
19. **GIFT SHOP/ NEWSTAND**
20. **AFT MEETING ROOM**

Marta, Sheemahant, Blackwood (if available), and seven soldiers are aboard the Riverine. The other eight soldiers are packed into the Otter. Each group also has a man-portable missile launcher with two AVMs (Intelligence 4, Ammo 2, Damage 12D8/6D4). The helmsman of each vessel and the gunners have a rating of 4 in the appropriate skill.

Also aboard the Otter are three metal cylinders about the size and shape of oil drums. Mounted on the top of each is a small electronic device with a keypad and LED display. These cylinders are bombs that Marta designed to deliver the Red Masque virus. Together the bombs carry enough virus to turn a 20-city-block radius into a dead zone. The electronic devices are the timers/detonators for the bombs. The timers are set for 2 hours, but will not be triggered until the bombs have been loaded aboard the *Queen*. (Two hours is the time it will take the *Queen of the North* to travel from the rendezvous to Kitimat's inner harbor.)

If the ferry reaches chart location F3-10.32.01/28.41.90 with the HNAL soldiers still in control of the vessel, it stops, and they winch the three viral bombs aboard, positioning them in the mountings installed during the voyage to the rendezvous. They then program the ferry's autopilot, set the timers on the bombs, and evacuate the vessel. The ferry should cruise at normal speed into Kitimat harbor. The bombs will detonate—bang, hiss—and tens of thousands of people are simultaneously infected by Red Masque and will die in a couple of days. The HNAL team will use the two smaller boats to return to their base on Hawkesbury Island. Mission accomplished. (They think. See **The Backup**, in **Picking Up the Pieces**.)

If the runners try to intercept Marta and crew before they reach the ferry, the Riverine will run interference for the Otter, using its weapons to hold off the runners' team until the bombs are loaded aboard.

A cautious team might wait until the bombs are aboard, then board the ferry and try to disarm the weapons. Not an easy job. The detonators are designed so that, once set, they cannot easily be turned off. A decker can try to hack into the electronics, assuming he or she has the appropriate interface hardware, but disabling the timers this way is very difficult, using a Target Number of 11. The timers feature a fail-safe anti-tamper mechanism. If someone tries to disarm them electronically and fails to get at least one success, then the timer mechanism "slags down," melting most of its internal circuitry, and making further attempts to disarm the timer impossible.

The HNAL soldiers have also booby trapped the mountings securing the bombs. Each emplacement is surrounded by four shaped-charge mines, similar to claymores, rigged with proximity fuses. Anyone or anything approaching within one meter of the emplacement triggers the mines. The charges explode outward, away from the viral bombs. The Damage Code is 7M3, with a reduction of –1 per 2 meters. The charges are also rigged with anti-tamper devices that will detonate the mines automatically if someone tries to disarm them. The viral bombs themselves are protected against astral or magical interference by Force 4 wards set by Sheemahant and Marta.

If the team manages to bypass, disarm, or survive these protective devices, they could just toss the bombs overboard. They could also reprogram the autopilot so that the ferry sails out to the open ocean. They should be reminded, however, that both these courses will cause an environmental catastrophe of unknown severity.

DEALING WITH THE VIRUS

For obvious environmental reasons, sinking the bomb-laden ferry, or the Otter while it is carrying the bombs, is a bad idea. The sea water would soon corrode holes in the metal cylinders, releasing the Red Masque virus into the ocean, with unpredictable, but probably unpleasant, consequences. The team needs to find a safe way to dispose of the virus.

Creative players will probably come up with a dozen innovative suggestions, but here are a few ideas, just in case.

•Hide the cylinders in a safe place, like a nuclear waste storage site. (Not ideal, because somebody might dig it up years from now. Also, radiation may transmute the virus into something even worse.)

•Incinerate the cylinders, possibly by magical means, hopefully destroying the virus at the same time.

•Develop a magic-based way to destroy the virus (for instance, a Kill Red Masque spell).

•Blast the cylinders with Turn to Goo (and hope that the goo is not infectious too. Keep in mind that this is a Sustained spell.)

•Fire the virus into space.

•Seal the cylinders in concrete and sink them in the ocean. (Again, not ideal.)

DEBUGGING

This encounter is the big one. Remember that Marta, Sheemahant, and the others are "true believers" in the cause, even if they work for different reasons. (See the individual descriptions in **Cast of Shadows**). They know their stuff, so they will not make any conveniently stupid mistakes, and they are willing to die for the cause. This encounter should turn into a rolling firefight, featuring lots of flying lead and many kilos of detonating high explosives. Pull out all the stops, describing in gory detail the heavy damage the team's weapons do to the good ship *Queen of the North*, or to anything else they cut loose at. After this episode, the runners should be glad to put their Panther assault cannons in mothballs, and be satisfied with "minor" weapons like Uzi IIIs. Encourage full-on "heroic" roleplaying here. Perhaps for the first time in their careers, the runners are fighting to save uncounted thousands of innocent victims. (Kinda gets you right here, doesn't it, chummer?)

Make sure the team sees this one through to its conclusion. A "tactical withdrawal" will almost certainly be considered an outright loss. The consequences of the team's failure are described in **Picking Up the Pieces**, p. 50.

The team might simply end up with three cylinders full of active Red Masque virus. As heroes, the runners will realize their duty is to destroy this horrible weapon in the safest, most efficient way possible. Certainly, they could turn around and sell the stuff; after all, many potential buyers will be interested in acquiring such an effective weapon. But the continued existence of a powerful viral weapon is not a good thing, even in the dystopian world of **Shadowrun**.

CONTACTS

To follow up on or discover clues in this adventure, the player characters need to investigate people, places, and situations. One of the best ways for runners to get the information they need is through their contacts. This section provides Success Tables containing information available to the runners from their sources.

A Success Test using Street or Corporate Etiquette, Target Number 4, typically serves to find out what a contact does or does not know. The amount of information available depends on the number of successes the player achieves. Characters who achieve more than one success gain all the information available to all previous levels of success.

The gamemaster should try to make the player character's interaction with his contact more than a few simple, abstract die rolls. The meeting should be played out in full: contacts are characters with their own lives, points of view, and needs, not simply spigots of information to be turned on and off automatically.

The player character should roll a number of dice equal to his Etiquette Skill to determine what information the contact knows and is willing to impart. Once the player character's number of successes is known, the meeting can take place, and the gamemaster can roleplay the encounter with the appropriate information level in mind. Meetings should be tailored to the "personality" of specific contacts. Some will want to have a straightforward meet in a specific place, others will have more elaborate forms of information exchange set up.

Contacts are generally considered trustworthy, as long as the runners play it safe. A player character should never compromise his contact by making it obvious that information came from him, or by revealing that the team may be planning to hit some group with which the contact is affiliated. Are the contact's ties stronger to his group or to the runner? A good runner never tests those ties by putting his contact in a situation where he must choose.

Whether or not the runner has to pay for his contact's services, and how long it will be before the contact may want information or a favor in return, can add another dimension to these encounters. Remember, most streets are two-way.

The information below is presented in the order the player characters are likely to encounter it.

THE KEMANO SUBSTATION RAID

Several nights before Farseer approached the runners, the HNAL staged a raid on a major electrical substation in a poor Kemano neighborhood. (This is the raid described in the **Prologue**.) Several missile hits destroyed the substation and set fire to many homes near the station. Only a fortuitous cloudburst allowed the fire to be controlled as quickly as it was. The official death toll of eight from the attack and fire is disputed; the actual figure is perhaps twice that. The government news service admits that the explosion and fire were the result of sabotage, but denies that the HNAL is responsible. (The government wants to deny even the sabotage, but that would mean that the explosion was spontaneous, which would reflect very badly on their Civil Engineering department.)

Appropriate Contacts (Target Number 4)

Any Street Contact in Kemano (if the contact is a member of the Tsimshian government, the Target Number rises to 6), or any Government/Political Contact with an interest in NAN/Tsimshian politics and events

Successes	Result
0	"Yeah, it was a big fire, took out one of the electrical substations. No power in the area for days. Eight people dead, apparently. Nobody knows what happened."
1	"Nobody's officially admitting what happened. Some kind of sabotage, that's for fragging sure. And the death toll's much higher than eight."
2	"I talked to someone who was there, and he says it was a fragging *missile* attack, chummer. Who the hell's going to be lobbing missiles around?"
3	"I'll tell you, it's that—whadda they call themselves?—the Haida National Army of Liberation or some such drek."
4+	"Some slag told me those HNAL guys hang out at this Kemano tavern called The Randy Sasquatch."

HAIDA NATIONAL FRONT (HNF)

The HNF is a covert organization dedicated to fighting oppression of the Haida and Kwakiutl peoples in the Tsimshian Nation. Initially, it tried to operate through political means. Some years ago, it turned to terrorist activities to achieve its goals. When the Tsimshian armed forces responded to these attacks with violence, killing large numbers of HNF members, the group reverted to its original non-violent, political tactics to try to bring about change in the nation.

Appropriate Contacts (Target Number 5)

Any Tribal, Media, or Government Contact (if the contact is in Tsimshian, the Target Number drops to 3)

Successes	Result
0	"Don't know, chummer. Native group, obviously, but I can't tell you anything specific."
1	"Oh yeah, those guys up in Tsimshian. Blew up a bunch of cop shops, then got the drek blown out of them by the local military types."
2	"Turned up a bloody mess some years back, lost a lot of people when the government went in with the big guns. But now it looks like they're back on the scene…"
3	"…and up to their old tricks again, blowing up stuff big time."
4	"At least, that's what most people think. The way I read it, there must have been some kind of schism. It's a splinter group that's going bomb-happy."
5+	"The new guys call themselves the Haida National Army of Liberation. Don't you just love revolutionary rhetoric?"

HAIDA NATIONAL ARMY OF LIBERATION (HNAL)

After the HNF was shot up by the Tsimshian military in retaliation for terrorist strikes, the group's surviving members returned to using less violent methods of achieving political change. Some HNF members, however, especially the young hotheads, decided that the military response called for additional violence, and split off to form the HNAL. Now the HNF is lying low, but the HNAL is blowing things up. Unlike the old HNF, the HNAL has no headquarters or home base. When they need to meet they do so in secluded, out-of-the-way areas such as abandoned warehouses, members' basements, and anywhere else secrecy can be guaranteed. Meeting locations change randomly to prevent the group from being compromised.

Appropriate Contacts (Target Number 6)

Any Tribal, Media, or Government Contact (if the contact is in Tsimshian, the Target Number drops to 4)

Successes	Result
0	"Who?"
1–2	"That's just a new name for the Haida National Front. Same people, different name."
3–4	"It's some kind of splinter group of the HNF. The HNF try to change governmental policy through political pressure. The HNAL try to change things through the injudicious application of gratuitous violence."
5–6	"The leader of the HNAL is some guy called Sheema-something. Sheema-hant, yeah, that's it."
7+	"I don't know if I buy this one or not, but I've heard rumors about some connection between the HNAL and those TerraFirst! loonies from CalFree."

DANIEL SHEEMAHANT

Daniel Sheemahant is a militant Haida. He joined the HNF at the tender age of 16, back when the group was heavily involved in terrorist activities. He earned himself a formidable reputation as chromed, smart, and downright nasty. He was one of the few survivors of the Tsimshian military's attack on HNF headquarters and bears the scars to prove it. He almost singlehandedly orchestrated HNAL's breakaway from the traditional HNF, serving as its unchallenged leader. His recent close association with Marta, leader of the northern arm of the TerraFirst! organization, appears to be drawing him more and more deeply under her influence. His leadership of the HNAL is currently nominal, at best.

Appropriate Contacts (Target Number 6)

Any Tribal, Media, or Government Contact in Tsimshian (if the contact is a member of the HNAL or TerraFirst! the Target Number drops to 4)

Successes	Result
0	"Sheemahant? He's dead, geeked when the Tsimshian army boys did a hard hit on HNF headquarters a couple of years back."
1	"One tough chummer. He somehow managed to get out of the HNF bloodbath. He must still be in the HNF, I guess—knowing him, he's probably the leader."
2–3	"Nah, he's not HNF any more. You heard about the HNAL, the Haida National Army of fragging Liberation? He's the bossman. A real hard one, too."
4–5	"Likes blowing things up, and very professional he is about it, too. His buddies like the same thing. The buzz on the street is he's hooked in real tight with TerraFirst!."
6+	"Close friends with that TerraFirst! slitch, Marta or something. Real close, get my drift? I think she's applying the old wrench, har, har, har."

TERRAFIRST!

TerraFirst! emerged in the late 20th century as low-level eco-terrorists, into spiking trees. The current incarnation makes Greenpeace—and even Greenwar—look like geriatric knitting circles. A group of hard-cases that only pay lip service to their ecological goals, TerraFirst! blows things up just to see the shrapnel fly. The main group is still based in California Free State, despite government attempts to stamp it out. A northern arm recently started operating in the Tsimshian Nation.

Appropriate Contacts (Target Number 6)

Any Media or Law Enforcement Contacts (if the contact is a member of the HNAL, the Target Number drops to 4)

Successes	Result
0	"TerraFirst!? Old news, chummer. The CalFree government killed them all off a year or so back."
1	"Eco-terrorists, real in-your-face types. Can't say I disagree with their goals—save the earth, stop pollution, that kind of thing—but I don't hold with their tactics. 'If it pollutes, blow it up,' that just isn't right."
2–3	"They're lying low in CalFree, but a northern arm has started stirring up trouble in Tsimshian."
4	"The leader's a shaman, name of Marta. Death on two legs, and wants everybody to know it."
5	"She's real close with the guy in charge of the Tsimshian HNAL. You know the group? I think the two groups are operating together…"
6+	"…and the way I hear it, they're working up something really nasty. When they do it, I don't want to be in the way."

MARTA

Marta is a Toxic Avenger shaman of the Dog totem. (See **The Grimoire**, p. 101, for information on Toxic shamans and Avengers.) As a Toxic shaman, she perverts the precepts of her totem and is a rabid, ravening destroyer of everything Dog would hold dear. This face she keeps hidden, however, presenting to the world a smooth operator with charisma to burn. Her powers, and certain cooperative Toxic spirits, informed her of the chem-bio weapons in the secret lab beneath Klawock. She plans to use them to wipe the Tsimshian region clean of its human "infestation." Through various means of influence, she gained control over Daniel Sheemahant, leader of the HNAL, and indirectly dominates that group as well as the TerraFirst! faction she leads.

Appropriate Contacts (Target Number 8)

Any Tribal or Law Enforcement Contact (if the contact is a member of TerraFirst! or the HNAL the Target Number drops to 5)

Successes	Result
0	"Who? Don't know her. Don't want to know her."
1	"Shaman. Dog shaman. Powerful Dog shaman. Nasty powerful Dog shaman."
2	"You know the group calls itself TerraFirst!? They've got a northern arm, operating in Tsimshian and the Athabascan Council. She's their leader."
3	"TerraFirst! is not a shy and retiring type of organization, you know what I mean? But under this Marta woman's leadership, the northern group makes their CalFree buddies look like conscientious objectors."
4	"She's hooked up with the HNAL—you know, that terrorist band led by Shimhunt, or whatever his name is. I hear the two groups are working together, and it's Marta who's calling all the shots. Bad news for Tsimshian, that's what I say."
5	"Real nasty and twisted, that one is. Always got a couple of real unclean spirits hanging around."
6+	"Toxic Dog shaman, that's the news as I hear it. Pretty bad, huh? Well, that's only half of it. I understand she's got her hands on some nasty new weaponry. And knowing what I know about Toxics, she won't be shy about using it."

THE RANDY SASQUATCH

This small tavern is in one of the more run-down sections of Kemano—needless to say, one of the sections inhabited almost exclusively by Haida and Kwakiutl tribe members. A rough, nasty, dangerous place, it is not a healthy atmosphere for an Anglo. The vast majority of regulars are Haida, and a good number are either members of, or sympathetic with, the Haida National Army of Liberation.

Appropriate Contacts (Target Number 4)

Any Street Contact in Kemano

Successes	Result
0	"The what sasquatch?"
1	"Oh, yeah. Yeah, I heard of that place. Down on the flats, near the river. North end of town."
2	"It's in the Haida/Kwakiutl neighborhood, a real rough part of town, if you get my drift…"
3	"…particularly if you ain't Haida. And particularly if you're an Anglo, Anglo."
4	"One piece of free advice: don't say anything against the HNAL if you want to stay out of a fight."
5+	"After all, odds are that at least a couple of HNAL members will be in there when you're flapping your lips."

WEAPONS LAB

At about the turn of the century, the U.S. military decided to ignore the international restrictions against research into chemical and biological (chem-bio) weaponry. (After all, evidence clearly showed that the Soviet Union had been flouting those restrictions for more than a decade.) Accordingly, the U.S. Army built a secret underground research lab near the town of Klawock, on Prince of Wales Island, just off the Alaska "panhandle" coast west of Ketchikan. When it became apparent that the U.S. would be forced out of Alaska, Army engineers planted enough explosives throughout the lab to level it. For some reason, several charges failed to detonate. Most of the lab was destroyed, but a significant portion of the lab, and presumably its contents, survived.

Appropriate Contacts (Target Number 8)

Any Military Contact

Successes	Result
0	"Don't know nothin' about it."
1–3	"Classified!" (The runners should figure that something is, or was, going on at Klawock.)
4	"You didn't hear this from me—it'd cost me my commission. But, yeah, the old U.S. military had a special weapons lab near Klawock. Real out-of-the-way place, on an island west of Ketchikan, Alaska. But they toasted that puppy real good when they pulled out. That lab's long ago history."
5	"Real nasty stuff. Chem-bio weapons. Nerve agents, genetically tailored viruses. Nice, huh?"
6+	"Ya know what? Couple of years ago, I talked to one of the Army engineers who did the torch job on the Klawock lab. He said the detonation he recorded wasn't big enough to account for all the explosives they packed down there. I don't know just what that means, but chummer, I don't think I like it."

RED MASQUE

Red Masque is the code name of a particularly nasty bioweapon: a viral agent that causes mental and physical deterioration in mammals, leading to eventual death. This was just one of the goodies created in the Klawock weapons lab.

Appropriate Contacts (Target Number 10)

Any Military Contact

Successes	Result
0	"What? Never heard of it."
1	"Oh, frag. I heard the name once, but I don't know squat about it. And, to tell you the truth, I don't want to know squat about it."
2	"Oh, man, where'd you hear that name, chummer? No, don't tell me, I don't want to know. It was a bioweapon, bucko, a real nasty one. But it's history…isn't it?"
3	"Red Masque? Frag, I should geek you just for mentioning the name. A real nasty virus, lethal, read me? The old U.S. buried that one real deep. It's not something they want anyone to know about."
4+	"You're playing with fire, chummer. That's an old project, something they were messing with at Klawock. Don't tell anybody that I told you."

CAST OF SHADOWS

LAURENSTEIN.91.

WALLACE BLACKWOOD

Wallace Blackwood was born a Haida in Kitimat in the Tsimshian Nation. His father, David Blackwood, was a member of the Haida National Front during Wallace's formative years. David was arrested and imprisoned for terrorist activity when Wallace was in his teens and was "shot while attempting to escape" soon after that. Wallace never bought this story, and believes the Tsimshian government murdered his father.

Wallace's family fell on hard times without his father's support, and his mother had to work two jobs to feed her children. To lighten her load, Wallace left home when he was only 16 and started working, sending most of each paycheck home. Wallace's life was rocked by tragedy a second time at age 20. The Tsimshian police force used live ammunition to break up a Haida/Kwakiutl demonstration, and his mother, an innocent passerby, was killed by a stray round.

Twisted and driven by hate, Wallace vowed to destroy the government that had killed his parents. He ran the shadows solo for a while, working at any job that would hurt the Tsimshian establishment. At age 26, he met Daniel Sheemahant, who persuaded him to join the revitalized HNAL. He is completely committed to the aims of the organization, and personally loyal to Sheemahant.

During his years on the street, Wallace met an Owl shaman who taught him how to come to terms with a magic potential that Wallace was completely unaware he possessed. He learned quickly and developed into a proficient, occasionally inspired Owl shaman. He is a Grade 4 Initiate.

Wallace Blackwood is a hard man, willing to kill in cold blood if he thinks it will further his goals. He has dedicated his life to the HNAL and to Sheemahant, and will gladly sacrifice it for the cause.

Blackwood has a constant spirit companion, always appropriate to the domain, of Force 3. If he is encountered in the underground lab, this will be a hearth spirit; if aboard the ferry, it will be an ocean spirit.

Attributes
Body: 4
Quickness: 4
Strength: 4
Charisma: 3
Intelligence: 5
Willpower: 4
Essence: 6
Reaction: 4
Magic: 6

Dice Pools
Astral (Defense): as Skill
Astral (Dodge): 5
Astral (Magic): 5 (10)
Astral (Special): 4
Defense (Armed): 5
Defense (Unarmed): 4
Dodge: 4
Magic: 5 (10)

Skills
Armed Combat: 5
Conjuring: 6
Etiquette (Street): 4
Etiquette (Tribal): 4
Firearms: 6
Magical Theory: 4
Sorcery: 5
Stealth: 3
Unarmed Combat: 4

CONDITION MONITOR			
MENTAL			
PHYSICAL			
L	M	S	D/UNC

Gear
Amulet (Power Focus 5)
Black Scorpion Machine Pistol [Light Pistol, 35 (clip), 3M2, w/Laser Sight]
Chemsuit over Armor Clothing (3/0)
Knife (2L1)

Spells
Combat
Manablast: 4
Powerblast: 5
Stunball: 4
Urban Renewal: 4
Detection
Combat Sense: 3
Totem: Owl, Grade 4 Initiate

Health
Resist Pain: 3
Illusion
Chaotic World: 5
Transformation/Manipulation
Personal Anti-spell Barrier: 3
Personal Physical Barrier: 3
Transform: 4

MARTA

Marta has only ever used that name. Her background, her upbringing, her birthplace, and all other personal information remains shrouded in mystery. The only fact that is obvious and undeniable is that she is not Amerindian. She first appeared on the scene some ten years ago as a member of the California-based TerraFirst! eco-terrorist group. Five years ago, she moved north and created the "chapter" of TerraFirst! currently operating in the Tsimshian, Athabascan Council, and Algonkian-Manitoo nations.

Marta is in her mid-30s, slender and attractive, with long, lustrous black hair. She has a winning smile, but close observation reveals that that smile never reaches her sea-green eyes. Despite her relatively slight build, she is exceptionally strong. A persuasive speaker, with great skills in rabble-rousing oratory, her voice becomes sultry and sexually charged in intimate surroundings.

When her TerraFirst! group initially began working with the HNAL, Sheemahant and Marta held equal responsibility, and had equal say in the combined group's operations. This has changed over time, however. Marta has influenced Sheemahant by all the means at her disposal, gaining control over the HNAL leader and so indirectly dominating the HNAL group as well as her TerraFirst! chapter. She is well aware that if Sheemahant escapes from her Influence and Control Emotion spells, he will reject her plan to release the Red Masque virus in Kitimat Harbor. The HNAL soldiers follow his orders, not hers, and she will kill Sheemahant before she will allow him to disrupt her plans.

Marta is a Toxic Dog shaman. As do all Toxic shamans, she perverts the basic precepts of her totem, acting as a rabid, ravening destroyer of everything Dog would hold dear. She keeps this evil hidden, however. As a Grade 4 Initiate, she is always accompanied by a Toxic earth or water spirit, depending on her location, of Force 5. In a fight, she gives no quarter and expects none, fighting to the death to bring her plans to fruition.

Attributes
Body: 3
Quickness: 5
Strength: 5
Charisma: 6
Intelligence: 5
Willpower: 6
Essence: 6
Reaction: 5
Magic: 6 (10)

Dice Pools
Astral (Defense): as Skill
Astral (Dodge): 5
Astral (Magic): 5 (11)
Astral (Special): 4
Defense (Armed): 3
Defense (Unarmed): 4
Dodge: 5
Magic: 5 (11)

Gear
Armor Clothing (3/0)
Necklace (Power Focus 6)
Orichalcum Knife [Weapon Focus 5, (2L1)]
Uzi III [SMG, 16 (clip), 4M3, w/Laser Sight and Gas-Vent Recoil System (2)]

Skills
Armed Combat: 3
Conjuring: 6
Etiquette (Street): 6
Etiquette (Tribal): 2
Firearms: 3
Leadership: 6
Magical Theory: 6
Psychology: 4
Sorcery: 5
Stealth: 4
Unarmed Combat: 4

CONDITION MONITOR
MENTAL
PHYSICAL
L   M   S   D/UNC

Spells
Combat
Manablast: 4
Powerblast: 5
Stunball: 5
Urban Renewal: 5
Wrecker: 4
Detection
Combat Sense: 3
Personal Clairvoyance: 5
Health
Resist Pain: 4

Illusion
Chaotic World: 5
Transformation/Manipulation
Control Actions: 3
Control Emotions: 4
Control Thoughts: 4
Influence: 5
Personal Anti-spell Barrier: 5
Personal Physical Barrier: 6
Totem: Dog (Toxic), Grade 4 Initiate
Threat Rating: 6*

*If Blackwood successfully removed the last of the Red Masque virus from the Klawock lab (in **Lab Work**) and delivered it to Marta, Marta's Threat Rating increases by +1. If she succeeds in sailing the bomb-laden ferry into Kitimat harbor, even if no one is killed by the virus, she receives an additional +1 to her Threat Rating. (This makes her considerably tougher if she comes after the runners for revenge, or if they try to track her down.)

DANIEL SHEEMAHANT

Daniel Sheemahant was born and raised in Tsimshian, a member of the Haida tribe and so part of Tsimshian's underclass. He joined the Haida National Front when he was 16 and rapidly rose to the top ranks of the organization. The Tsimshian government's attack on the HNF headquarters led Sheemahant to orchestrate the breakaway of the more militant Haida National Army of Liberation (HNAL). He remains, officially, at least, its unchallenged leader. He is a tall man, almost 2 meters in height, well muscled and exceptionally strong. He is skilled in the use of a large number of personal and heavy weapons, and a lethal in-fighter.

Since meeting Marta over a year ago, he has fallen steadily and increasingly under her spell. His followers in the HNAL do not know that he is permanently under the influence of Marta's Control Emotions and Influence spells, which she placed in spell locks on his person. If these spells were removed, he would vehemently repudiate Marta's plan to release the Red Masque virus in Kitimat Harbor. (Marta knows this, of course, and will take the necessary steps to keep her plan in motion.) While under her influence, he would give his life to see her plans through to completion and to save her from harm.

Attributes
Body: 5 (8)
Quickness: 4
Strength: 5 (7)
Charisma: 6
Intelligence: 4
Willpower: 4
Essence: 1.35
Reaction: 4

Dice Pools
Defense (Armed): 4/6/8
Defense (Unarmed): 6
Dodge: 4

Skills
Armed Combat: 4
  Concentration: Edged Weapons 6
  Specialization: Combat Axe 8
Demolitions: 6
Etiquette (Street): 4
Etiquette (Tribal): 6
Firearms: 4
  Concentration: SMGs 6
  Specialization: HK 227 SMG 8
Gunnery: 4
  Concentration: Machine Guns 6
Leadership: 5
Military Theory: 2
Motorboat: 3
Stealth: 5
Throwing Weapons: 2
Unarmed Combat: 6

Cyberware
Cyberlimbs [both arms w/Increased Strength (2) and Retractable Spurs, Smartgun Link (right)]
Dermal Plating (3)
Low-Light Cybereyes w/Flare Compensation

Gear
Four IPE Offensive Aerodynamic Grenades (6S4)
Two Spell Locks holding Influence and Control Thoughts (cast by Marta)
Combat Axe [Concealability 2, Reach +2, Damage 2 (3)S2]
HK 227 [SMG, 22 (clip), 5M3, w/Gas-Vent Recoil System (2) and Built-in Smartgun Link]
Knife [2(3)L1]
Micro-transceiver

CONDITION MONITOR
MENTAL
PHYSICAL
L   M   S   D/UNC

FARSEER

Farseer is an eagle shapeshifter. Born in the Canadian wilds just after the Awakening, she is as attached to the land as her spirit cousins. Through means and channels unknowable by man, she has learned of the horror that Marta threatens to unleash on the land. She has vowed that Marta will not succeed, but the world of the Toxic shaman will always be hidden from Farseer. To stop a human, she must use humans.

Frightened and confused by the cold plasticrete world of Seattle, Farseer displays many of the animal traits she seeks to conceal from the runners. Her head cocks to one side when she listens. Her eyes are in constant motion, her attention darting from person to person. She would rather fly free in the open spaces—the dark backrooms and shadow-laden lives of runners are not to her liking.

If needed, Farseer can be the gamemaster's ace-in-the-hole, but that is what Tael is for. If the player characters need both non-player characters to aid them, they deserve little in the way of reward.

The first number listed below for each attribute is Farseer's rating in her true, eagle form. The second value is for her shifted human form.

Attributes
Body: 3 (3)
Quickness: 8x4 (6)
Strength: 7 (3)
Charisma: 6 (6)
Intelligence: 3 (3)
Willpower: 3 (3)
Essence: (8) (dual being)
Reaction: 5

Powers
Enhanced Physical Attributes
Regeneration

Weaknesses
Allergy (Gold, Severe)
Vulnerability (Gold)

CONDITION MONITOR			
MENTAL			
PHYSICAL			
L	M	S	D/UNC

PICKING UP THE PIECES

THE FALLOUT

If the team successfully stopped the viral bombs from detonating, they can return to Seattle and to the Blue Flame Tavern, where Farseer awaits them. With congratulations, she hands over the balance of the fee she promised, also in fist-sized nuggets of pure gold. No matter how the team orchestrated their success, the Tsimshian government will never officially recognize that any danger of this magnitude existed. Attempts by the shadowrunners to force recognition of their deeds in order to claim some form of reward will be met with stolid silence at best, or imprisonment for "criminal rumor-mongering" at worst.

If the team solved the problem by tossing the viral bombs into the ocean, sailing the bomb-laden ferry into open water, or detonating the viral bombs themselves, Farseer will not hand over the reward. She explains angrily that, though they might have completed the mission to their satisfaction, it was not completed to hers. The bioweapon was released into the environment, with incalculable damage to life in the region. The runners surely cannot expect any kind of reward for such dubious "success."

Marta and Sheemahant may still be alive and on the loose. Sheemahant is never heard from again; Marta kills him off because his usefulness is at an end. Without his charismatic leadership, the HNAL loses momentum and eventually rejoins the moderate HNF. Marta and her TerraFirst! colleagues will continue to plan and execute miscellaneous acts of war against the Tsimshian region over the next several years. The team should try to keep a low profile, or Marta may come after them looking for revenge. If Marta lives, her activities can be the basis for many future adventures.

THE BACKUP

What happens if the team fails in a big way and is unable to stop the bomb-laden ferry from completing its voyage into Kitimat harbor? Do the bombs detonate, killing countless thousands of innocent victims?

As a matter of fact, no. A backup team was in place to prevent this hideous eventuality. One of the significantly powerful Tsimshian secret societies had its own source of information and its own plan. A shamanic group calling itself the Skinwalkers (the name is from their tradition of wearing headdresses made from the skins of symbolically powerful animals) knew about Marta's plans. Between the time that Marta's crew loaded the bombs aboard the *Queen of the North*, and the ferry arriving in Kitimat, several Skinwalkers and their spiritual companions visited the vessel and magically neutralized the virus. (How is not important, because nobody but the gamemaster will ever know that this is what happened. Maybe they developed and used a Slay Virus spell.) In any case, the detonators went off, severely damaging the ferry and releasing an aerosol into the atmosphere. This aerosol was biologically inert, however, so no casualties resulted.

If the team survived the adventure but failed to stop the bombs from reaching Kitimat, they may be interested in finding out exactly what happened. Let them try. The Skinwalker secret society will be very difficult to track down, and future adventures can be based on the team's attempts to track down the city's saviors.

AWARDING KARMA

Apart from the reward offered by Farseer, should they earn it, this adventure provides for little monetary reward. The potential Karma windfall, however, should more than make up for that lack. Award Karma to each player according to the following events:

Marta dies	5
Sheemahant dies	2
Blackwood does not remove the virus from the lab	2
The viral bombs do not explode in Kitimat	6
The viral bombs are safely destroyed	4
The viral bombs detonate	−2
The bombs are thrown overboard, or the vessel carrying them sinks	−1
Selling the virus	−1

Individual Karma awards should be made at the gamemaster's discretion.

PLAYER HANDOUTS

TODAY'S HEADLINES:
Compiled by T. Gallagher

INTERNATIONAL
• Severe electrical storms disrupted telecommunications, Matrix operations and electrical power in much of Québec Nation Friday. Many areas were still without power late Saturday morning.

• A United Kingdom government spokesman acknowledged 37 arrests at equinox celebrations at Stonehenge, but denied reports of widespread rioting and major supernatural happenings.

LOCAL
• Several paranormal new boars caused havoc in downtown Seattle Friday morning. Boars were reported in 11 different locations, but police were only able to round up four. It is not known if those four were responsible for all sightings, or how they came to be downtown.

BUSINESS
• Five Japanese corporate officals commited suicide together Thursday. Their employer, KAN-Triangle, is expected to post massive losses for the third quarter. The suicide may simply be a reaction to the losses, or a sign of deeper trouble at KAN-Triangle.

ENTERTAINMENT
• The underwater-gladiator trideo genre may have run its course. Public reaction to the long-awaited, big-budget *Manta 4, Ray of Revenge*, has been tepid.

SPORTS
•Friday night's game set an NFL record for futility, as the Minnesota Vikings lost to the Orlando Thunder by an astounding score of 103-6.

BIG RUMBLE IN LITTLE JAPAN?
M. Colton

International District—Lone Star Security reports recent evidence of an apparent clash between two rival factions in the area. Several bodies were discovered in an abandoned warehouse following an anonymous tip to Lone Star. A spokesman for the security company blames the deaths on local gang activity.

Desk Sergeant Toku Yoshihiro stated, "This is simple go-gang hooliganism." The sergeant denied any yakuza or Mafia involvement in the slayings.

Informed sources, however, connect these killings to the recent disappearance of local Japanese businessman, Tokugawa Tetsuo. Mr. Tokugawa has not been seen since Friday. The same sources allege that Mr. Tokugawa is an up-and-coming yakuza officer.

TSIMSHIAN FERRY DELAYED
N. Findley

Yesterday's run of the Port Hardy to Kitimat ferry service arrived three hours late in the Tsimshian Nation's capital, due to mechanical problems with the diesel turbine engines. "The ship could have pressed on at full speed and arrived on time," explained Derry Thomas, spokesperson for the Tsimshian Ferry Corporation, "but overstraining the damaged engine risked causing more extensive damage, which would have delayed the arrival even more. Our passengers expect, and deserve, on-time service. The captain, rightly, in our view, decided to arrive three hours late rather than risk being delayed up to eight hours by repair work." The problem was apparently a faulty bearing on one of the propeller shafts. Tsimshian Ferry Corporation is investigating the failure, and legal action against the bearing manufacturer is being considered. The commanding captain was unavailable for comment.

CHAMPION DETHRONED!
A. Lucas

Las Vegas—Pitfighter "Jackman" Davis lost to the surprise challenger "Stringer," who KO'd the champ eight rounds into the "Light Dance" bout, so named for the motion-tracking auto-guns mounted at each ringpost.

The match broke the previous endurance record set during the now-famous Troll Brawl last August in Berlin. Renraku Entertainment owns the exclusive license to the Jackman-Stringer fight and will release a simsense chip of the match next Tuesday.

FREIGHTER IN DISTRESS
W. G. Smith

Seattle—Metroplex Guard helicopters responded to a pre-dawn distress call today from the *Adelaide Mistress*, which lost power off Maury Island in Puget Sound. The Guard choppers rescued over three hundred people from the disabled freighter. Owners of the vessel refused to comment on why the ocean-going *Adelaide Mistress* was so dangerously overcrowded.

'DEAD ZONE' RUMORS DISMISSED
N. Findley

"This talk about a 'Dead Zone' is just typical overreaction by the news media," states Bernice John of the Tsimshian Environmental Service. "There is no dead zone. The area in question is home to a number of migratory species. When an area's animal population migrates away from that area, is the area automatically considered a 'dead zone'? No. It's simply the way nature works." See the Editorial section for a comment by Nature Correspondent Jameson Bathgate.

TODAY'S HEADLINES:
Compiled by T. Gallagher

INTERNATIONAL

• Severe electrical storms disrupted telecommunications, Matrix operations and electrical power in much of Québec Nation Friday. Many areas were still without power late Saturday morning.

• A United Kingdom government spokesman acknowledged 37 arrests at equinox celebrations at Stonehenge, but denied reports of widespread rioting and major supernatural happenings.

LOCAL

• Several paranormal new boars caused havoc in downtown Seattle Friday morning. Boars were reported in 11 different locations, but police were only able to round up four. It is not known if those four were responsible for all sightings, or how they came to be downtown.

BUSINESS

• Five Japanese corporate officals commited suicide together Thursday. Their employer, KAN-Triangle, is expected to post massive losses for the third quarter. The suicide may simply be a reaction to the losses, or a sign of deeper trouble at KAN-Triangle.

ENTERTAINMENT

• The underwater-gladiator trideo genre may have run its course. Public reaction to the long-awaited, big-budget *Manta 4, Ray of Revenge*, has been tepid.

SPORTS

•Friday night's game set an NFL record for futility, as the Minnesota Vikings lost to the Orlando Thunder by an astounding score of 103-6.

BIG RUMBLE IN LITTLE JAPAN?
M. Colton

International District—Lone Star Security reports recent evidence of an apparent clash between two rival factions in the area. Several bodies were discovered in an abandoned warehouse following an anonymous tip to Lone Star. A spokesman for the security company blames the deaths on local gang activity.

Desk Sergeant Toku Yoshihiro stated, "This is simple go-gang hooliganism." The sergeant denied any yakuza or Mafia involvement in the slayings.

Informed sources, however, connect these killings to the recent disappearance of local Japanese businessman, Tokugawa Tetsuo. Mr. Tokugawa has not been seen since Friday. The same sources allege that Mr. Tokugawa is an up-and-coming yakuza officer.

TSIMSHIAN FERRY ACCIDENT
N. Findley

Yesterday's run of the Port Hardy to Kitimat ferry service almost ended in tragedy when a fault in the vessel's autopilot caused it to crash into a service dock in Kitimat Harbor. "There was a fault in the electronics, yes," comments Derry Thomas, spokesperson for the Tsimshian Ferry Corporation, "but that does not absolve the vessel's captain of responsibility for this debacle. As captain, it is his duty to ensure that all systems aboard his vessel are in full working order. If the autopilot fails, he should be available on the bridge to take immediate corrective action. He failed to do so, and so the responsibility for this accident lies entirely with him. Captain Charles James has been relieved of his position, pending further investigation. We may press criminal charges." Captain James was not available for comment.

CHAMPION DETHRONED!
A. Lucas

Las Vegas—Pitfighter "Jackman" Davis lost to the surprise challenger "Stringer," who KO'd the champ eight rounds into the "Light Dance" bout, so named for the motion-tracking auto-guns mounted at each ringpost.

The match broke the previous endurance record set during the now-famous Troll Brawl last August in Berlin. Renraku Entertainment owns the exclusive license to the Jackman-Stringer fight and will release a simsense chip of the match next Tuesday.

FREIGHTER IN DISTRESS
W. G. Smith

Seattle—Metroplex Guard helicopters responded to a pre-dawn distress call today from the *Adelaide Mistress*, which lost power off Maury Island in Puget Sound. The Guard choppers rescued over three hundred people from the disabled freighter. Owners of the vessel refused to comment on why the ocean-going *Adelaide Mistress* was so dangerously overcrowded.

'DEAD ZONE' RUMORS DISMISSED
N. Findley

"This talk about a 'Dead Zone' is just typical overreaction by the news media," states Bernice John of the Tsimshian Environmental Service. "There is no dead zone. The area in question is home to a number of migratory species. When an area's animal population migrates away from that area, is the area automatically considered a 'dead zone'? No. It's simply the way nature works." See the Editorial section for a comment by Nature Correspondent Jameson Bathgate.

DANCHCHEKKERS PRIMER ON THE NATIVE AMERICAN NATIONS VOLUME TWO

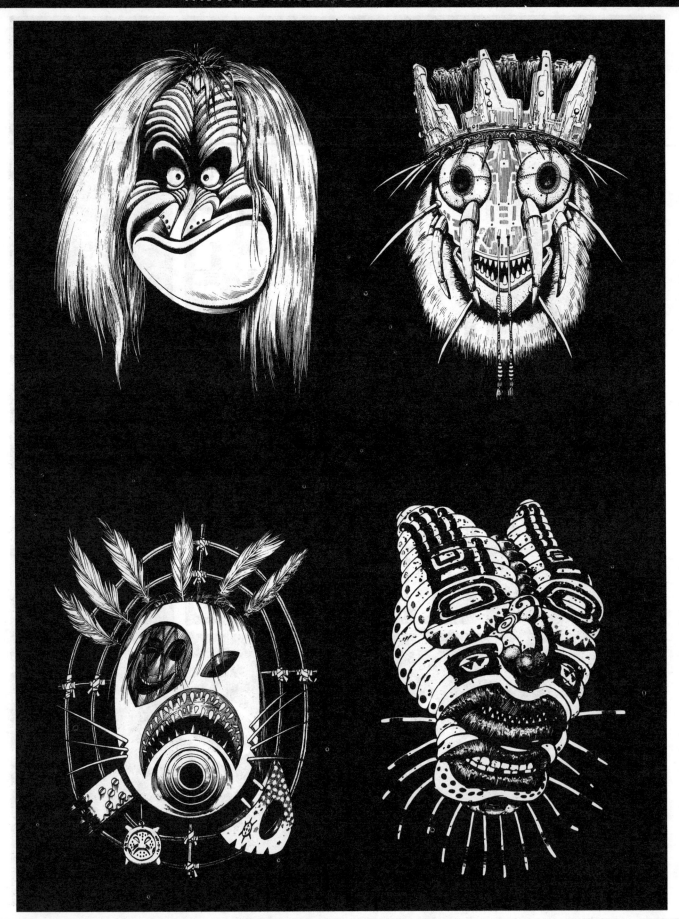

NATIVE AMERICAN NATIONS

INTRODUCTION

Welcome to the on-line version of *Danchekker's Primer on the Native American Nations, Volume Two*. This volume serves as a guide to understanding the traditions, economy, laws, people, and other aspects of the Algonkian-Manitoo Council, the Athabascan Council, the Trans-Polar Aleut Nation, and the Tsimshian Nation.

As with all the volumes in the *Danchekker's Primer* series, this book supplements and expands on the tribal-lands information included in most senior-high and university-preparation level courses. This information will be of value to students of sociology, anthropology, history, international relations, and government studies. Once again, it must be stressed that the *Danchekker's Primer* series is a supplement to—not a substitute for—standard classroom instruction and database research. Though this *Primer* contains information drawn from the standard reference works on the subject, the student should read those reference works for him- or herself.

The reader will note that this volume gives some prominence to events occurring in the 19th century and earlier. The reason is that, as a culture, Amerindians are bound more closely to their history than any other group in the world. Amerindians weave their past into the fabric of their present cultural traditions.

Every effort has been made to ensure the accuracy of this material, but the Native American Nations are dynamic, constantly changing entities. Danchekker's Primer Series Inc. accepts no responsibility for damage or loss resulting from information contained herein.

>>>>>[As with all of the "Danchekker's Primer" series, it's my considered advice that you trust the information contained herein about as far as you can spit a rat.

Good old Dr. Danchekker, friend to millions of lazy students. Why read the original reference works, why attend classes, when you can absorb it all in comfortably pre-digested form from the "lips" of kindly Dr. Danchekker?

If you can access this, welcome to the shadow edition of "Danchekker's Primer." I love this guy Danchekker, you know? Or I would if he really existed. "Danchekker" is actually five researchers and three copywriters, all rolling in nuyen thanks to the success of that kindly persona, Dr. David Danchekker.

And that revelation, oh my friends, is just an example of the deep background you will find in this, the shadow edition. I and my associates will endeavor—as "Dr. Danchekker" might put it— to elucidate the more erroneous statements in the standard edition. If you've got the computing wherewithal, feel free to update our comments, because—as we have been informed— "the Native American Nations are dynamic entities." On the other

hand, we take no responsibility for the accuracy of any of these third-party comments, either. Believe at your own risk...but you in the shadows know all about that.

Go to it, and leave no stone unturned. You'll be surprised at the creepy-crawlies you will find.]<<<<<
—Captain Chaos, Northwest Neo-Anarchists League (23:38:15/8-3-51)

>>>>>[Okay, if you scanned Volume 1 of this thing, you'll recognize the above as basically the same comments I made there. Hey—they're still relevant. If you haven't scanned Volume 1, give it a try. It's just as full of entertainingly wrong-thinking drek as this present opus. Enjoy, boys and girls.]<<<<<
—Captain Chaos (17:33:06/1-10-52)

GENERAL HISTORY

The Native American Nations did not exist prior to the signing of the Treaty of Denver in 2018, but the events that made the founding of NAN inevitable had begun some 50 years earlier. During the 1980s and 1990s, tribal groups across North America began filing land claims against the governments then in power. These claims demanded that the tribal lands usurped when the "white man" (Anglos) spread westward across the continent be returned, or else that financial restitution be made. In most cases, the governments deeded back to the natives at least a portion of the lands that once were theirs, unable to pay the compensation the tribes demanded.

This trend was reversed during the first years of the 21st century. Under pressure from the megacorporations, which had gained true extraterritoriality with the Shiawase Decision of 2001, both the United States and Canadian governments began invoking the right of eminent domain and repossessing the lands granted to the native tribes only a decade or so before. Megacorporations and coalitions of (relatively) small companies such as National Oil were granted licenses to exploit the repossessed lands for their oil and mineral resources.

Needless to say, the native Americans to whom these lands belonged did not take kindly to this land grab, dubbed by the media "The Resource Rush." Angry and frustrated, the more radical elements founded the Sovereign American Indian Movement (SAIM). SAIM made their point by blockading important highways, a tactic also used by Canadian Amerindians in the early 1990s. The first blockade was negotiated to a peaceful settlement. When the tribes protested a second time with blockades, the Canadian and U.S. governments, backed by the security forces of various corporations, simply took them out in the most efficient manner possible. The casualties were surprisingly low (except in the Mohawk confrontation), but the swift paramilitary response sent the leaders of SAIM an important message: the conflict had escalated.

The flashpoint came in 2009, when United Oil Industries announced that it had acquired the right to exploit the petrochemical resources in one-quarter of the remaining federal parks and one-tenth of the Indian lands, which the government had just confiscated. SAIM reacted immediately and decisively. A small band of commando-trained Amerindians—some of them one-time members of the USMC "Scalpel" Special Forces team—penetrated the Shiloh Launch Facility in northwest Montana, capturing the silo and gaining launch control of the 16-warhead "Lone Eagle" MIRV missiles within.

Issuing a demand for the return of all Indian land, the Shiloh raiders threatened to launch the silo's missiles. After ten days of tense negotiations, a U.S. Armed Forces "Delta" Crisis Response Team entered the silo complex. The penetration team "neutralized" the occupying force, but not before a single Lone Eagle missile was launched toward the Soviet Union.

Though the missile's warheads never detonated, there was still considerable fallout from the incident. When the North American public learned of the Lone Eagle crisis, the outcry was enormous. Goaded by corporate propagandists, the people began to blame SAIM, and by implication, all Native Americans. Lobby groups for the major corporations used the public outcry as "grassroots support" for their private agendas and pressured the U.S. government into passing the Re-Education and Relocation Act. (The Nepean Act, legitimizing similar camps, was signed into law in Canada on the same day.) These Acts called for anyone connected in any way to SAIM to be confined in so-called "re-education camps." Violent public hatred of Native Americans sent many thousands of Amerindians who had no connection with SAIM to the camps "for their own protection."

In a government economy measure, Congress and the Canadian Parliament contracted out management of the re-education camps to the corporations. Once the media spotlight was off the camps, conditions deteriorated drastically. Overcrowding, poor sanitation, and insufficient medical care became the standard. The camps were virtual gulags, cut off from the rest of North American society. (Ironically, it was this very isolation that saved the Amerindians when VITAS swept the world in 2010.)

The next major act in the Amerindian drama took place on December 24, 2011. Daniel Coleman, later Prophet of the Great Ghost Dance, led his followers out of the Abilene Re-Education Center. The guards opened fire on the natives as they walked to freedom, but no casualties were reported.

After Coleman led his cadre of believers out from the Abilene REC compound, he dropped from public view for several years. Knowledge of his activities during that period is minimal, but it later became obvious that he was spreading word of his power. Native Americans, both those who were free and those incarcerated in camps or restricted to the ever-shrinking reservations, heard of a new prophet, a great shaman to whom the spirits had taught a powerful dance. These tales inspired others to escape from the camps and to wage a guerrilla war against their enemies—the U.S. and Canadian governments and the corporations. As their ancestors had a century and more ago, the Native Americans struck fast and hard, then faded back into the wilderness. Unlike their ancestors, they had access to the same technology as their enemy. They also wielded the powers of magic, powers that the Anglos had yet to admit existed.

In 2014, Daniel Coleman, now calling himself Howling Coyote, stepped out of the shadows. Backed by an elite core of fanatics, he announced the formation of the Native American Nations, a coalition of tribes. The NAN laid claim to all of North America, and demanded the immediate withdrawal of all persons of European, African, and Asian ancestry. NAN threatened magical retribution if their demand was not met.

The NAN's demands were ridiculed by the media and ignored by the government. Then Redondo Peak erupted, burying Los Alamos, New Mexico, under a cloud of ash. Howling Coyote appeared in a vid-cast from a nearby Zuñi reservation, claiming credit for the disaster. The U.S. government reacted quickly, attempting to capture the self-proclaimed shaman by sending the Sixth

Air Cavalry Battalion from Fort Hood, Texas. The assault team never reached its destination. Violent storms tore their aircraft from the sky, and by the time a second force was mobilized, Howling Coyote was long gone.

The guerrilla war escalated. The armed forces and corporate armies of Canada, the U.S., and Mexico failed to stop the raiders.

The U.S. passed the Resolution Act of 2016 to resolve "the Indian question" once and for all. The plan was total extermination of all Native American tribes. (No corresponding legislation was ever passed in either Canada or Mexico. Both governments simply gave corporate forces tacit approval to take whatever actions they saw fit. The two countries could thus claim that they had never legislated genocide—though the results would certainly be the same.)

While the government and corporate forces planned their strategies for elimination, the followers of Daniel Howling Coyote planned their own strategy of resolution. The Great Ghost Dance began in 2017, as men and women of the tribes all across the continent performed the ritual Howling Coyote had taught them. They sang his songs and chanted his chants. Their power grew.

Freak weather and other uncanny disturbances disrupted troop and equipment movement, pushing back "H-hour" for what is now known as "The Genocide Campaign." Finally, however, the government and corporations across North America were ready to mobilize their forces. At 10:30 A.M. PST, August 17, 2017, the operation began to roll.

At 10:32 A.M. PST, Mount Hood, Mount Rainier, Mount St. Helens, and Mount Adams all erupted in cataclysmic fury. The Genocide Campaign ground to a halt. The Amerindians had made good on their threats, and no one could doubt their power again.

At the same time, Native American tribesmen and non-Indian sympathizers occupied military bases in all three North American countries, demanding a multinational conference. Chastened and wary, the three governments sent representatives to Denver to negotiate with the Ghost Dancers. In 2018, the results of the negotiations were formalized in the Treaty of Denver.

In the treaty, the federal governments of the United States, Canada, and Mexico acknowledged the sovereignty of the Native American Nations (NAN) over most of western North America. The document outlined a ten-year population adjustment plan that would relocate all non-Indians off lands belonging to NAN. Provisions included the establishment of reservations for non-tribal peoples and corporations, the maintenance of Seattle as an extraterritorial extension of the United States, and the division of Denver between various signatories to the Treaty.

The Treaty of Denver failed to satisfy any of the parties involved, but the signatories could not agree on another alternative. The Treaty still stands as one of the best examples of compromise in the history of political conflict.

Legitimized at last, NAN named Daniel Howling Coyote as head of the Sovereign Tribal Council, NAN's governing body. Though he found it difficult to mediate among the bickering that now began between various factions, Howling Coyote was probably the only man who could still rally the loyalty of all sides. Without an external enemy to unite the tribes, the internecine squabbles grew more intense, particularly over the issue of the

Awakened—the orks, dwarfs, trolls, and, most particularly, the elves—whom the tribal nations generally welcomed. In 2035, a major schism opened between the Tsimshian Nation and the other members of NAN. Two years later, the elves of the Northwest announced the birth of Tir Tairngire (the land of promise) and seceded from NAN. Emboldened by the elves' move, Tsimshian also officially seceded in 2037. This second blow to the unity of the STC intensified the internal strife. Unable to maintain the solidarity of the organization he had brought into existence, Daniel Howling Coyote, Prophet of the Great Ghost Dance, resigned his position and withdrew from society.

Since then, internal dissention has settled down to a form of background noise. The members of the STC recognize the Council's importance mainly as a rallying point for the different nations and a vehicle to coordinate action, should another outside threat to NAN ever materialize. Each individual nation has its own form of government, social structure, and social mores. The STC has not been granted the power to meddle in tribal affairs, however, and probably never will be.

FACTS AT A GLANCE

Population: 22,548,000
- Human: 56%
- Elf: 26%
- Dwarf: 7%
- Ork: 6%
- Troll: 4%
- Other: 1%

Per Capita Income: 17,000¥
Population Below Poverty Level: 23%
On Fortune's Active Traders List: 0%
Corporate Affiliation: 19%
Education:
- High School Equivalency: 54%
- College Equivalency: 25%
- Advanced Studies Certificates: 9%

Regional Telecom Grid Access: NA/ALM

CLIMATE

The Algonkian-Manitoo Council land comprises much of what once was western and central Canada. Spring and fall are considered by far the most pleasant times to visit this region. During the summer, temperatures are generally uncomfortable, often exceeding 32 degrees Celsius. The western portions of the Council enjoy the dry heat characteristic of prairie, but the eastern regions suffer from severe humidity, which combines with the high temperatures to create almost unbearable weather. The northern reaches of the Council are plagued by hordes of black flies and other nuisance insects when the temperatures soar.

>>>>>[Sometimes they're more than a nuisance. Reports say that some of the nasty little bloodsuckers can carry VITAS-like viral infections. This problem exists exclusively in the northern regions, however.]<<<<<
—Dan the Man (16:21:10/6-19-52)

Winter temperatures can drop to well below zero. In the western regions, the cold is often accompanied by strong winds, leading to significant wind-chill factors (–60° C effective temperature is not unheard of). Snow is common from late November to early March, with significant falls often occurring both earlier and later.

ACCESS

Plane

A large international airport is located in Saskatoon, the Council capital. Regularly scheduled flights connect to most of the large cities of the North American continent. Small commuter flights connect Saskatoon with other cities in Algonkian-Manitoo.

>>>>>[Regular flights…but they're always late.]<<<<<
—Barrab (18:57:55/3-17-52)

>>>>>[Compared to other parts of NA, the security checks at the airport are a fragging joke. "No, officer, that's not a heavy pistol, it's a cigarette lighter." "Thank you, sir. Please move along." Idiots.]<<<<<
—Steel Rat (04:38:47/3-19-52)

>>>>>[If they're such idiots, how do you explain the fact that the per capita rate of violent crime in A-M is among the lowest on the continent? Hm?]<<<<<
—Darth (11:02:49/4-7-52)

Automobile or Bus

Highway 1, once the Trans-Canada Highway, runs into the Algonkian-Manitoo Council from the UCAS to the southeast and from the Salish-Shidhe Council to the west. In the Sioux Nation, Freeway 15, once I-15, is a direct path north to the border of Algonkian-Manitoo, but once the road crosses the border, its quality decreases drastically. Whippet Bus Lines runs regular service from Winnipeg, in the UCAS, to Saskatoon.

TRIBAL DEMOGRAPHICS

The major tribes in the Algonkian-Manitoo Council are Algonkian, Ojibwa, and the tribes of the Iroquois group (with the notable exception of the Mohawk tribe), with minor populations of Navaho and Apaches. The approximate breakdown of the tribally aligned population is as follows:

Algonkian	40%
Ojibwa	23%
Iroquois	21%
Navaho	10%
Apache	5%
Other	1%

About 92 percent of the total population is tribally aligned. The remaining 8 percent is non-tribal and/or non-Amerindian. The majority of the non-tribally aligned population are "Anglos" who live on the land in the native way (or what they perceive to be the native way). Known as "pinkskins," they have organized themselves into tribal or sub-tribal groups and usually show stronger "back-to-the-land" tendencies than do the true natives, with the exception of some Inuit. The Algonkian-Manitoo Council government gives the pinkskin tribes very little voice, though no overt discrimination against pinkskins, or against non-Amerindians in general, exists.

Government positions are held almost exclusively by the Algonkian. The majority of the Ojibwa and Iroquois have chosen to take little or no direct part in the government of the Council. They represent a significant silent majority, however, and the government gives even their private opinions serious consideration in all decision-making. In fact, many highly placed council chiefs trust unofficial Ojibwa or Iroquois advisors in all matters of import.

No overt friction exists between the different tribes. The lack of Ojibwa and Iroquois presence in the government is by choice, not by any Algonkian manipulation.

>>>>>[Danchekker isn't really big on this kind of stuff, but it's interesting to examine the military and police set-up in A-M. The Council has strong, well-organized armed forces, all volunteer and overwhelmingly Apache. Same with the police forces. Good thing for the government that there *isn't* any tribal friction, because the Apache would be in a good position to stage a military coup should they ever feel the need.]<<<<<
—Matrix Samurai (13:33:33/6-13-52)

>>>>>[I made the tactical error once of entering into an alcohol-fueled difference of opinion with several Apache army-boys in a tavern. No chrome, they were straight off the rack, but they still fragging near tore my head off.]<<<<<
—Hawk (10:00:17/7-21-52)

>>>>>[Don't underestimate the Iroquois, either. They're quiet, polite people, until you insult them. Then they'll kill you. And remember, an insult is in the ear of the recipient...]<<<<<
—Holly (14:44:48/7-22-52)

>>>>>[The Iroquois tribes are interesting from a sociological standpoint. As Holly said, they're very quiet, seemingly well-balanced people. But I think there's some kind of racial inferiority complex operating under the surface, because many Iroquois become shamans. A large number of shamans are also "back-to-the-landers," people who give up the trappings of technology to one degree or another, try to recreate the traditions of their ancestors. Among this group, soon after a child reaches puberty, he or she goes on a "vision quest," looking for a spirit guide. The vision quest has many settings, sometimes the wilderness, sometimes the inner city, sometimes (I hear) even the Matrix. Those who find a guide become shamans. The back-to-the-landers also distinguish themselves by the way they wear their hair: both sexes wear two braids, often decorated with feathers.]<<<<<
—People Watcher (11:49:34/7-24-52)

>>>>>[The Ojibwa are quiet, usually avoiding all forms of physical and emotional aggression. Nice folks.]<<<<<
—Holly (15:51:14/7-27-52)

The Algonkian-Manitoo Council is made up of 26 percent elves, the highest percentage in any North American nation other than Tir Tairngire. Though some 15 percent of the elves are of Amerind ancestry (born of Native Americans), the vast majority of these "Indian elves" have withdrawn from the tribes of their heritage and have formed elven tribal groups. Elves in general show a strong "back-to-the-land" mentality. They believe technology interferes with an individual's connection to nature, and so should be minimized. This attitude is echoed by many in the Council, but the elven population seems particularly militant about it.

HISTORY AND CULTURE

The Algonkian-Manitoo Council has a diverse mix of cultural elements. The significantly large tribes (i.e., those who make up more than 5 percent of the population) come from three different cultures and geographic regions: the Far North (Algonkian), Eastern Woodlands (Ojibwa, Iroquois), and the Southwest (Navaho, Apache). The Algonkian, Ojibwa, and Iroquois are native to the land claimed by the Algonkian-Manitoo Council, while the Navaho and Apache contingents migrated here during and after the land-claim conflicts that created the hell of the re-education camps. The resulting historical and cultural blend is unique.

Historically, the Indians of the Far North region were hunters and gatherers. The tribes consisted of many small bands, usually related by marriage, each inhabiting its own territory, uninhibited by tribal chiefs. These tribes had good relationships with the white settlers from the beginning of the European influx, especially with the French fur traders. This relationship changed their way of life. They moved away from the old ways of subsistence and concentrated on trapping fur-bearing animals, whose pelts they traded to the Europeans for food, weapons, and more traps.

>>>>>[Sounds great, huh? Just trap a few small furry critters, and the French will keep you in the manner to which you want to become accustomed. In fact, this move eventually led to their downfall. Before the Europeans arrived, tribes in the Far North didn't fight each other, mainly because there wasn't that much to fight about. The fur traders brought the tribes into competition with each other. They started to war on each other as an extension of their competition for the fur trade with the Hudson's Bay Company and other outfits. They lost any kind of unity they might otherwise have had, and this cost them when the settlers started to move into their territory in force.]<<<<<
—People Watcher (10:17:18/6-12-52)

>>>>>[That's just how the fragging Anglos planned it when they started the fur trade.]<<<<<
—Kaska (18:14:51/6-18-52)

>>>>>[Doubtful.]<<<<<
—Holly (06:39:18/6-28-52)

In the wars between the French and the English, the Far North Amerindian tribes fought on both sides of the conflict.

During the late 1500s, five Eastern Woodlands tribes, the Cayuga, Onondaga, Oneida, Mohawk, and Seneca, joined together to form the Iroquois Nation under the leadership of the great Mohawk chief Hiawatha. This nation controlled the northeastern region, around the state of New York, for almost two centuries. The European settlers encountered the Eastern Woodlands tribes first. Relations were initially good, but quickly broke down as the Europeans claimed larger and larger tracts of land for themselves. War broke out and lasted for decades. Though the Amerindian tribes fought courageously, and they were vastly outnumbered, outcome was a foregone conclusion. Tribes moved west or north, or were relocated onto reservations.

During the war with the Europeans, the Iroquois Nation broke up into its individual tribes again, and pursued individual goals. In the late 1980s and early 1990s, the Mohawk tribe came to the fore, a militant group intent on reclaiming its ancestral lands. Bands of Mohawk warriors set up blockades across major roads and fought strongly against anyone who tried to enter their reservations.

>>>>>[Not quite, Danchekker. The battles in the '90s weren't some noble attempt to reclaim their homelands. The Mohawks had set up some very profitable racketeering on their reservations, and they were fighting to make sure the governments of Canada and the U.S. didn't take that away from them.]<<<<<
—Lucy (15:57:10/3-20-52)

>>>>>[LIES!! Poisonous Anglo lies.]<<<<<
—New Hiawatha (15:26:13/3-26-52)

>>>>>[Sorry, chummer, Lucy's right—at least partially. The profitable racketeering business was a major reason for the early squabbles, particularly the nastiness around Oka, Kahnawake, and Kanesatake in Québec in 1990. But around 1996, the Mohawks cleaned house, geeked the racket bosses, and started to pursue their land claims properly.]<<<<<
—Skeleton Hunter (15:08:16/4-25-52)

The history of the Mohawk tribe is discussed in detail in *Danchekker's Primer on the Native American Nations, Volume One.*

With the founding of SAIM, the tribes that once comprised the Iroquois Nation regrouped, believing that a unified federation would fare better in the coming conflict. Since reforming, the member tribes of the nation have made an effort to subsume their individual identities into the united Iroquois Nation.

>>>>>[Simplistic as always, Danchummer. The tribes are confederated, but they *haven't* completely given up their individual identities, although, granted, the differences aren't that great on the surface. But call a Seneca a Cayuga—both Iroquois tribes—and you've got trouble on your hands, believe me.]<<<<<
—People Watcher (23:04:52/3-10-52)

>>>>>[What about the Mohawks? I've skimmed *Volume One*, and they're listed as an independent tribe in the Sioux Nation.]<<<<<
—Toby (01:00:29/5-8-52)

>>>>>[After the second Kahnawake conflict in 1999—the one in which the Canadian army went in with missiles (see *Volume One*)—the Mohawks were shifted to a secure "Protection Center" near Swift Current, Saskatchewan. The U.S. government sent their Mohawks there as well, to keep them out of trouble. This is why there are no Mohawks among the Algonkian-Manitoo Council Iroquois.]<<<<<
—People Watcher (23:20:17/5-9-52)

>>>>>[There are some, People Watcher, but not many. They came north and east after things had settled down, that is, after the formation of the Algonkian-Manitoo Council and the Sioux Nation. They seem to have integrated quite well into the Iroquois tribe, though some of them are on the militant side.]<<<<<
—Holly (22:42:13/5-21-52)

The history and culture of the southwestern tribes is discussed in detail in *Danchekker's Primer on the Native American Nations, Volume One.* Small groups of Navaho and Apache were relocated to the north during and immediately after internment in the re-education camps, and many elected to remain on the Algonkian-Manitoo Council lands as citizens.

Many members of the Iroquois, Ojibwa, and Algonkian wear traditional garb on festive occasions or at tribal ceremonies. Traditional dress is deerskin shirts, leggings, and breechcloths. The Algonkian usually fashion their traditional costume from the skin of moose or caribou.

>>>>>[There's a smattering of back-to-the-landers who wear this kind of stuff all the time. They are generally Iroquois, and very proud of their heritage. You won't slot around with these guys if you know what's good for you. And if you're interested in finding out about *real* back-to-the-land fanatics, check out the next section.]<<<<<
—Holly (16:48:49/2-17-52)

A TRIBE IN PERSPECTIVE: THE MANITOO

A relatively large network of anti-technology elves has emerged in the last two years in the Algonkian-Manitoo Council land. This group calls itself the Manitoo tribe ("Manitoo" is Algonkian for elf) and is petitioning the government for official recognition. The Manitoo strongly oppose technology that pollutes or represents a potential eco-hazard, or that they consider intrusive to an environmentally sound lifestyle. Though the majority of Manitoo believe these issues can be effectively dealt with by political means, lobbying, petitions, and so on, a small, disaffected faction within the tribe has threatened to use more extreme measures.

>>>>>[More than threatened, Danchummer. You're talking about the Manitoo Brotherhood, a real radical group of anti-technologists who respond to "inappropriate" technology by blowing the drek out of it. They bombed a GMC plant last year, killed fifteen workers. They hit a Litton Industries plant in January just because

they heard the company put out guidance modules for long-range tacnukes. (What makes it worse is that they were wrong.)]<<<<<
—Wahoo Murphy (05:29:20/3-22-52)

>>>>>[The group that bombed the Litton Industries facility was not officially part of the Brotherhood. They call themselves "the Squamish Five," to commemorate a similar action carried out some 70 years ago. Though the members of the Five may consider themselves members of the Manitoo Brotherhood, we repudiate them. The Litton facility was non-polluting, and therefore not directly harmful to the land. The Manitoo Brotherhood's wrath is directed at such polluters as the GMC manufacturing plant that poured millions of liters of poison into our lakes and rivers.]<<<<<
—Manitoo Eagle (02:48:22/4-17-52)

>>>>>[Neo-Luddites!]<<<<<
—Technocrat (22:00:25/5-6-52)

The formation of the Manitoo tribe is an interesting study of the effects of UGE on a homogeneous society. The majority of Manitoo come from Algonkian-Manitoo Council tribes. Though some of these tribes and bands accepted Awakened members, many did not.

>>>>>[This wasn't an official position, of course—the tribal leaders didn't say, "Elves out!" or anything. It was more a matter of individual xenophobia, which you see everywhere in the damn world.]<<<<<
—Todd (18:03:17/7-2-52)

The elves felt uneasy and unwelcome at the change UGE wrought and left their tribes or bands, wandering the country as tribeless "lost ones." Even in tribes and bands where the Awakened were accepted, even welcomed, many elves felt out of place. UGE had changed more than their appearance, and they no longer felt at one with their heritage.

The elven lost ones would have continued to wander alone through the Algonkian-Manitoo Council lands if a charismatic leader had not appeared to bring them together. This leader was a young elf named Adrienne Silvermoon (Adrienne Jim). Born an Iroquois elf, she left her tribe soon after puberty.

▼ ▼ ▼ ▼ ▼ ▼ ▼

Silvermoon attended a New York university as one of the few exchange students who benefited from a short-lived UCAS policy of educational cooperation, and earned her degree in social psychology. During her time at university, she became involved in a fringe back-to-the-land and anti-technology movement and emerged as an influential member of the radical TerraFirst! group. Her great charisma and rabble-rousing public speaking skills helped her rise to a position on the council of the TerraFirst! East Coast chapter. Her attitudes proved too radical, however, and she was removed from power.

>>>>>[Too radical for TerraFirst!? That's pretty fragging radical.]<<<<<
    —Jodi (18:28:40/2-6-52)

>>>>>[TerraFirst! policies go in cycles. They're radical as hell at the moment, but at that time they weren't into blowing up power plants and drek like that. And Adrienne Silvermoon was. More on that later.]<<<<<
    —Skeleton Hunter (15:38:08/3-2-52)

When she returned to her tribe, Silvermoon realized that the "lost ones" represented an opportunity for her to accomplish her private agenda. She single-handedly set in motion a campaign to bring the disaffected elves together under the banner of a new tribe, which was the Manitoo. Her campaign was wildly successful.

>>>>>[Of course it was. Look at the psychology involved. Her pitch was that the elves' greatest loyalty was to the land and to others who loved the land as they did. In a single stroke, it turned the elves' alienation from their tribes into a noble act on their part, a turning away from the safe and traditional to a cause of global importance. No surprise that a drekload of elves immediately jumped onto her bandwagon.]<<<<<
    —Holly (08:04:08/2-24-52)

The Manitoo tribe grew quickly, and became a focus for the back-to-the-land movement in the Algonkian-Manitoo Council. After several years as its leader, Adrienne Silvermoon stepped down and retired into obscurity.

>>>>>[Danchekker repeats the sanitized version. Here's what really happened. When she was setting up the Manitoo, Adrienne Silvermoon had to back off from her militant attitudes. When she was building up membership, she sounded completely rational, making noises about appropriate technology, minimal environmental impact, conservation of resources, concentration on renewable resources, and so on. This was the same pitch that Greenpeace used before they went rabid—remember "Greenwar"?—and it was just what the people wanted to hear.
    Once she had the membership numbers up to where she wanted them, she shifted into her real agenda. This was, in essence, no technology, mankind is a blight on the planet, and let's start blowing stuff up. Some hotheads among the Manitoo liked this, because sabotage was a good way of livening up a dull

Sunday afternoon. But the majority recognized that this was not the way to go. They attempted a political ouster of Adrienne. Most of the leaders of this political move died in weird, supernatural ways. Adrienne claimed this was the spirits of their ancestors punishing them for turning aside from their destiny, but not too many Manitoo bought this line.
    The next coup attempt, instigated by the only survivor of the first try, was a different story entirely. This was a real coup, with armed warriors and a couple of shamans providing backup just in case. The precautions were warranted. Adrienne refused to give up her position and tried to geek the delegation that had come to request her resignation. A really nasty magical battle ensued, and quite a few people bought the farm. From what I hear, Adrienne bought it herself when she tried to call up one last spirit. She blew the call and it had her for lunch. No body was ever found.
    Leadership of the Manitoo fell to the leader of the coup, a guy who took the name Derek Highsun (probably to reinforce a contrast with Adrienne Silvermoon). He's a rational bleeder, and the Manitoo are pursuing quiet, back-to-the-land policies in their own territory, instead of working globally.
    The question of the Manitoo Brotherhood remains. Unsubstantiated but recurring rumors say that Adrienne Silvermoon is behind that fringe looney group. If so, the reports of her death must have been greatly exaggerated. If true, the Brotherhood is more dangerous than most people think.
    Oh, yeah, I did some research on Adrienne herself, and I consider the evidence incontrovertible: Adrienne Silvermoon was, or is, a Toxic shaman. And if you know what that means, you know why I say the Brotherhood is real dangerous.]<<<<<
    —Skeleton Hunter (17:24:36/3-2-52)

ECONOMY

The Algonkian-Manitoo Council operates on a light- to medium-level industrial economy. Saskatoon and Grand Rapids are the industrial centers of the nation, with factories turning out a line of low-cost cars (notably the Manitoo and the Arcadian) and a variety of light to heavy construction machinery and vehicles. Daiatsu-Caterpillar has opened a major plant in Red Lake, and Yokogawa has commissioned a nearby plant to develop modular structural units for heavy construction. Significant political opposition exists to any proposed growth in the manufacturing segment, and the government is considering new, more stringent laws governing waste emissions.
    The western portion of the Council is largely agricultural, concentrating on growing genetically engineered strains of grain such as neo-triticale and stonewheat. The nation's income is largely based in the sale of grain to other North American countries.

>>>>>[Two years ago, attempts to genetically engineer improved nitrogen fixing for these grains almost wiped out all the crops. Seems the microorganisms they built fixed nitrogen like gangbusters, but gave off some waste products that decreased the viability of the root systems they were implanted in. The local gene-splicers had to call in Aztechnology to build them a virus specific to the new microorganisms. Must have cost them a pretty penny, if I know Aztechnology.]<<<<<
    —Dr. Frank (14:02:36/4-18-52)

>>>>>[What it cost them was an open-ended contract under which Aztechnology "supervises" all future genetic engineering work relating to the grain crops. Translation: Monopoly position for Aztechnology.]<<<<<
—Pyramid Watcher (04:30:15/4-28-52)

The standard of living in the Algonkian-Manitoo Council is best described as "comfortable." Though average wages are lower than in other parts of North America, so are prices.

>>>>>[Here's the stuff you really want to know: cost differentials between A-M and the conventional baseline (i.e., Seattle).

ALGONKIAN-MANITOO COST OF LIVING	
ITEM	COST
Weaponry	
Ammunition	100% (1)*
Explosives	— (3)
Firearm Accessories	120% (2)
Firearms	90%
Melee Weapons	60%
Projectile Weapons	80%
Throwing Weapons	60%
Armor and Clothing	
Armor	90% (4)
Security and Surveillance	
Communications	100%
Security Devices	100%
Surveillance Countermeasures	150%
Surveillance Measures	120%
Survival Gear	70%
Vision Enhancers	130%
Lifestyle	
Lifestyle	70%
Electronics	
Electronics	100%+ (5)
Cybertech	
Biotech	95%
Bodyware	130%
Cyberdecks	300% (8)
Headware	130% (6)
Internals	130% (7)
Programs	200% +
Magical Equipment	
Hermetic Library	100%
Magical Supplies	80%
Magical Weapons	100%
Power Foci	70%
Ritual Sorcery Materials	100%
Spell Foci	70%
Vehicles	
Aircraft	120% (9)
Boats	90%
Ground Vehicles	85%
Military Vehicles	— (10)

*Cost of Living Notes

(1) Non-belt-fed, non-explosive rounds only. Belt-fed or explosive rounds are unavailable—officially—without a government permit. You can get them from shadow sources, but the price is whatever the market will bear (i.e., make sure your credstick's real healthy).

(2) Silencers and smartgun links are available only in the shadows; expect to pay a hefty premium.

(3) Totally unavailable (officially) without a government permit, and those aren't easy to get. Check the shadows. Costs are typically slightly more than what you want to pay.

(4) We're talking light body armor only, here. Security-grade or military armor is available only through shadow channels from the boys in the army, or the corps. Knowing the corps, you're better off trying the army.

(5) Varies, depending on the sophistication. Remember, A-M isn't technology oriented, meaning that the real wiz stuff has to be imported.

(6) Ditto electronics.

(7) And again.

(8) You'd be better off trying to track down hen's teeth. Bring your own.

(9) All imported.

(10) Yeah, well…you don't buy this stuff, chummer. If you need it, "borrow" it.

Notice the way this works? High tech is costly and hard to obtain.]<<<<<
—The Keynesian Kid (17:06:45/2-11-52)

>>>>>[There used to be a channel into the military where you could get some of the more lethal toys. Unfortunately, the main fixer stiffed the wrong customers, and they blew him up—and his warehouse, and his friends, *and* a good chunk of downtown Lloydminster.]<<<<<
—Hangfire (19:18:08/2-22-52)

>>>>>[The pattern of corporate presence is interesting. You've got the big boys, MCT, Renraku, and recently Aztechnology, but not too many of the other multinationals. I don't know why; maybe they don't consider the markets big enough to bother with.]<<<<<
—Jobu (08:41:24/3-3-52)

>>>>>[Take a look at the ownership of the "local" corps and you'll see what's happening. Telecommunications, much of manufacturing, and almost all of the entertainment industry is owned indirectly by the multinationals.]<<<<<
—Sly (12:04:14/3-6-52)

>>>>>[Anchorage-based Athabascan Oil and Northern Light Plastics (really one and the same) also have a large presence.]<<<<<
—Polly Glot (15:13:42/3-12-52)

>>>>>T-bird run! BTL chips, some cyberdecks, and other tech-toys. If you're a drek-hot rigger and don't mind a little heat, we're looking for you. Frog Hollow Net Mailbox 10187, Toronto, UCAS (leave message).]<<<<<
—Ramrod (22:19:28/4-1-52)

GOVERNMENT

The Algonkian-Manitoo Council's governmental system is based on a Cheyenne tradition dating back several centuries. Three separate chiefs lead the tribe: a civil or "peace" chief, a war leader, and a ceremonial leader.

>>>>>[An interesting aside. Note the government structure is based on Cheyenne tradition, but there's no significant Cheyenne population in the nation. This is another good example of the borrowing and mixing of cultural traditions that's gone on since even before the Great Ghost Dance.]<<<<<
—People Watcher (15:54:31/7-22-52)

>>>>>[Goshers, that Great Ghost Cha-Cha just shook everything up, eh? Wonder who taught 'em?]<<<<<
—Minstral (17:15:51/7-23-52)

>>>>>[Please, let's not start this again.]<<<<<
—Sweet Mary (04:12:10/7-24-52)

The civil leadership is a hereditary position, held for life, inherited patrilinearly through the Bear family (Algonkian tribe). The civil chief is responsible for administering the civil service, including the national police force, and acts as arbiter in meetings between the war chief and the ceremonial chief.

>>>>>[Currently it's Robert Bear, a Bear shaman.]<<<<<
—Eagle (18:27:49/3-30-52)

>>>>>[Though Bobby Bear is nominally in charge of the police force, the guy with the real clout in that area is David Longmiles. Apache, of course, and a real ironsided son-of-a-slitch. Incorruptible and too smart by half.]<<<<<
—Silver Surfer (23:04:02/4-2-52)

The war leader is selected by the joint chiefs of staff of the nation's armed forces. The office is held for a four-year term.

>>>>>[…and there's no limit to the number of consecutive terms. The war-boss is an Apache named Carl Hillborn, and he's in his fourth term of office. This boy is chromed to the max, and I think he did at least one tour in Desert Wars.]<<<<<
—Eagle (18:30:10/3-30-52)

The ceremonial leader is elected by popular vote and serves a five-year term. All national policy decisions must be agreed to by all three chiefs.

>>>>>[Ceremonial leader is Laura Hawksford, Algonkian. Very popular, and coming up for re-election soon.]<<<<<
—Eagle (18:32:56/3-30-52)

>>>>>[Don't let her sweetness-and-light facade fool you, chummers. She's harder than Longmiles. A Snake shaman, she's exceptional at illusion-type stuff.]<<<<<
—Silver Surfer (23:09:52/4-2-52)

LAWS

IMMIGRATION

Customs and immigration checks at the borders of Algonkian-Manitoo are swift and efficient, conducted by polite and friendly border guards. Delays at the border rarely last more than half an hour.

>>>>>["…conducted by polite and friendly border guards" who kept a couple of Ares Predators leveled at my head while their buddies stripped my car.]<<<<<
—Cap'n Crunch (13:07:19/4-22-52)

>>>>>[It couldn't have anything to do with the fact that you're a chromed troll with a Tokogawa-era samurai top-knot, could it? Nah…]<<<<<
—Bung (18:45:46/4-30-52)

Citizens of the bordering nations, the Athabascan Council, Salish-Shidhe, Sioux, UCAS, and Québec, do not need visas to enter Algonkian-Manitoo Council territory. Other Amerindian nationals may be required to show travel passes. Contact your local Algonkian-Manitoo Council embassy for details. Visitors who want to work while in Algonkian-Manitoo must obtain a work visa, available directly from the Ministry of Labor in Saskatoon. Applications may be made in person or electronically.

>>>>>[A-M is short of skilled labor in many of the high-tech fields. When Canada fell apart, most of the brains went to Québec (if they could speak French) or south to the UCAS. So if you're good at what you do, don't sweat the work visa. People will hire you anyway—the visa program is just a rubber stamp. I have yet to hear of an application being rejected.]<<<<<
—Captain Chaos (00:14:27/3-30-52)

Only citizens of the Algonkian-Manitoo Council may make their permanent residence there (permanent is defined as more than six months in any calendar year). Applicants for citizenship must either prove that their lineage includes one of the major tribes of the area or be sponsored by a Council-based corporation. Sponsored applications are considered only if no current citizen of the Algonkian-Manitoo Council has the required skill-set.

>>>>>[Finding a sponsor isn't usually a problem. See above.]<<<<<
—Captain Chaos (00:15:14/3-30-52)

Not all permanent residents of the Council are of Amerindian descent, of course. When the Council was established, the area's current residents were allowed to choose between accepting citizenship or moving. The majority decided to stay on, retaining their old jobs and ways of life. In the intervening years, however, Amerindians have filled most positions of authority in both the public and private sectors.

CIVIL AND TRIBAL LAWS

The nation's legal system is based on the British adversarial system, and so will be familiar to residents of the UCAS and most other North American nations (with the notable exception of Québec). All judges are shamans of Amerindian extraction, the government's single major concession to the nation's tribal nature. The law treats all citizens and visitors even-handedly.

The Algonkian-Manitoo Council land is mostly rural, made up of small towns. Reflecting the seemingly universal nature of small-town life, national laws against firearm possession are typically lax, and rarely strictly enforced.

>>>>>[True, but only when it comes to hunting weapons, or bang-bangs that might be used as hunting weapons. The law still comes down heavy on people packing assault rifles, smartguns, and drek like that. (You don't hunt food game with a Panther Assault Cannon or an Uzi III and smart goggles.)]<<<<<
—Tommyknocker (10:35:52/7-1-52)

>>>>>[Fines and sentences for most crimes are on a par with what you'd get in the UCAS, Seattle included.]<<<<<
—Legal Beagle (19:46:54/7-22-52)

Several laws drawn from tribal traditions may seem strange to UCAS citizens. For example, polygamous marriages (one man, several women), are legal and common.

>>>>>[Hoo-hah!]<<<<<
—Randy (09:44:40/3-8-52)

>>>>>[Marriages also are common between cousins.]<<<<<
—People Watcher (05:02:59/4-28-52)

In addition to civil law, most sub-tribal groups maintain traditional disciplinary systems that deal with "social" transgressions committed by members of their specific groups. Local tribal councils handle cases in which tribal mores or taboos that do not transgress civil law are broken. The councils mete out punishments ranging from fines or community service to banishment.

>>>>>[The interesting thing here is that these councils' decisions aren't legally binding. The convicted person may reject the punishment assigned. Of course, the consequences of rejecting a sentence are severe. The accused will be shunned forever by the tribal group, and very few transgressors are willing to face that punishment. In a sense, punishment is self-imposed.]<<<<<
—People Watcher (05:08:18/4-28-52)

>>>>>[This is definitely true within the Manitoo.]<<<<<
—Tinuviel (11:20:08/5-14-52)

INTERNATIONAL RELATIONS

The Algonkian-Manitoo Council enjoys exceptionally good relations with all other nations in North America except Tsimshian. The Council has strong reciprocal trade bonds with the UCAS, the Republic of Québec, and the Sioux Nation. A small export trade has been established with the Trans-Polar Aleut Nation.

>>>>>[The A-M has a strong voice on the NAN Sovereign Tribal Council. The current representative is an Algonkian named Mary Nightwind, a Dog shaman. She's highly respected inside the A-M and out, and speaks with a refreshing voice of reason among more highly strung Council reps.]<<<<<
—Gaia (18:57:37/5-20-52)

>>>>>[I hear that the Athabascan Council is petitioning the NAN to change the national boundaries. The way I get the story is that the Athabascans want the northern end of the A-M Council land as far south as the town of York Factory (yup, that's its real name, and it's been around for about a century) near Cape Tatnam on Hudson Bay. (God knows why, there's nothing of any value in that stretch of real estate.) Needless to say, the NAN backed Nightwind over the Athabascan rep. Could be some bad blood there.]<<<<<
—Lounge Lizard (21:02:28/5-22-52)

▼ ▼ ▼ ▼ ▼ ▼

The Algonkian-Manitoo Council has cordial relations with nations outside North America, but close ties to none. It sends a representative to the North Atlantic Economic Organization (NAEO) meetings in The Hague, but has no special relationship with any NAEO members.

>>>>>[…and we all know how effective NAEO is on the world stage, don't we?]<<<<<
—Bung (22:51:58/6-25-52)

GENERAL COMMENTS

As with all NAN nations, the present Algonkian-Manitoo tribal population has a far different makeup than the population before 2010, a result of the tribal mixing in the re-education camps. When the Native Americans were released from the camps, many requested transport to areas far from their historical homes. They simply wanted to escape the scene of so much humiliation and so many bad memories.

>>>>>[Requested? Well, I suppose a few did. But the whole relocation process was a bureaucratic nightmare. Originally, people were shipped to camps far from their homes because the governments of their home regions considered them "subversive elements" to be separated from other "potential militants." When it came time to leave the camps, many were told that their homes and businesses had been confiscated by the government, and that they had no home to go back to. Some stayed where they were; others were asked to choose another homeland. Those who stayed in the camps when the rest of us walked out registered for relocation to their homes, but somehow the paperwork ended up in the wrong files. Their resettlement papers sent them to Port Alberni, Tsimshian, for example, instead of Port Allegany, UCAS. Danchekker doesn't mention this problem much in the rest of the *Primer*, but it's important that exactly what happened to us be understood.]<<<<<
—John (19:06:38/1-27-52)

The Algonkian-Manitoo Council is a pleasant place to visit. The citizens are friendly and polite, and visitors are welcome. As when taking in the local color anywhere else, tourists should respect local tribal customs.

>>>>>[Skipping back to the comments inserted earlier about the position of non-native-owned business in A-M, Pyramid Watcher made a good point in his entry on 4-28. Since Aztechnology came to the rescue in the nitrogen-fixing incident, it's been trying to extend its foothold beyond its monopoly on the genetic-engineering field. It's been casting acquisitive glances at locally owned industry in other investment and development segments, and the grapevine carries whispers of Aztech using high-pressure tactics to gain equity positions in local corporations. Even without the equity-position situation, the local corps have begun to realize how much competitive clout Aztechnology can bring to bear in *any* business segment, now that it's established.

Popular reaction to this incursion is building. A couple of weeks ago, an Apache youth got gunned down by Aztechnology corp-cops when he spray-painted "Aztechnology Out!" on the corporate HQ in Saskatoon. The grass-roots sentiment is that the government should revoke Aztechnology's monopoly on biotech and expel them from the nation. Stay tuned for further developments.]<<<<<
—Manta (11:11:34/9-15-52)

>>>>>[And it goes even deeper. The buzz I hear says the government might bow to public opinion and try to nationalize the Aztechnology holdings.

Yeah, right. I used to work for Aztechnology's security arm, and I know what their response would be. The Big A is not what you'd call adverse to political interference. Just ask the Panamanian government that got itself purged last year. If the Algonkian-Manitoo government tries to push Aztech around, Aztech will shove back, hard. And if it comes to a scrap, my ex-colleagues can field an army the same size as and better equipped than the A-M forces. Remember, Aztechnology's unofficial motto is "Don't step on me or I'll tear off your fragging head and spit in your neck (and I just might do it for fun anyway)."]<<<<<
—Ex-Corporate Warrior (20:16:59/9-17-52)

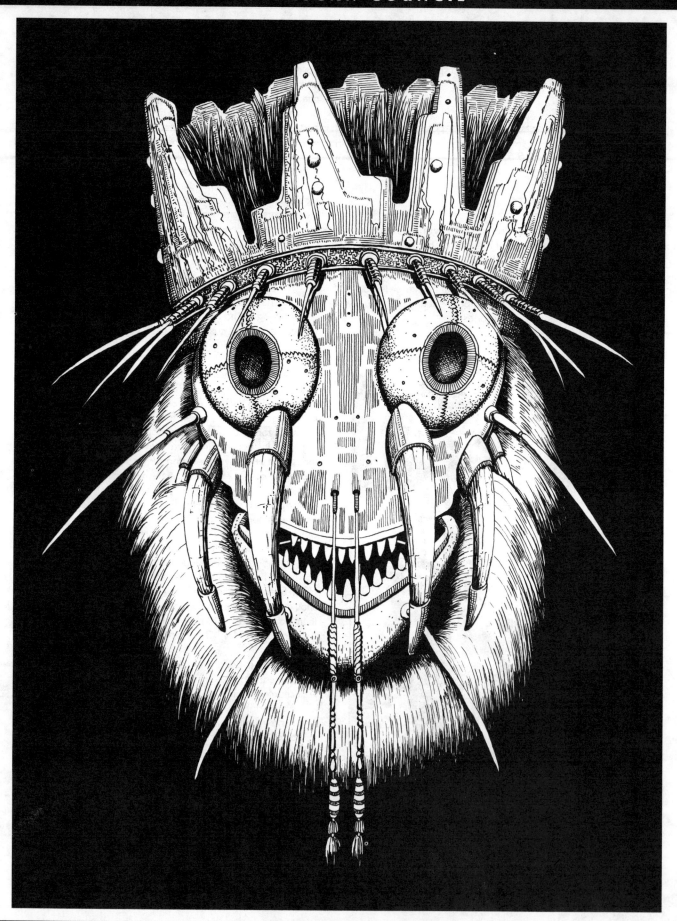

ATHABASCAN COUNCIL

FACTS AT A GLANCE

Population: 14,398,000

Human:	70%
Elf:	8%
Dwarf:	8%
Ork:	9%
Troll:	5%
Other:	0%

Per Capita Income: 16,000¥
Population Below Poverty Level: 25%
On Fortune's Active Traders List: 0%
Corporate Affiliation: 10%
Education:
High School Equivalency: 48%
College Equivalency: 18%
Advanced Studies Certificates: 3%
Regional Telecom Grid Access: NA/ATH

CLIMATE

Much of what was once Alaska and the Yukon, as well as some of northern British Columbia and the Northwest Territories, now make up the Athabascan Council. Summer is undeniably tourist season. On the coast, daytime temperatures reach 24 degrees Celsius, dropping at night to 10° C or less; inland, the range is more extreme, from 30° C down to 5° C. The warmer inland temperatures bring out hosts of black flies and other nuisance insects.

>>>>>[See my entry under the A-M Council. Insect repellent is highly recommended.]<<<<<
—Dan the Man (16:46:34/6-19-52)

Winter temperatures drop to well below 0° C; the climate is even colder when the wind chill is factored in.

Most of the Athabascan Council territory lies close to or within the Arctic Circle, which means the number of daylight hours varies considerably throughout the year. The far north regions experience several weeks of "white nights" in mid-summer, when the sun never drops completely below the horizon. The remaining summer nights are only fully dark for a few hours. In mid-winter, there are several weeks when the sun never rises at all and night seems almost perpetual.

Snow prevails for six months of the year, and frequent storms blow in off the Gulf of Alaska.

>>>>>[Weather conditions are more extreme now than they used to be, according to the records I've been scanning. Storms are fiercer and more common. Alarmists claim that the weather disruptions result from the geothermal plants that the SovUnion's been sinking into the sea bed under the Arctic ice cap. I think that's probably drek.]<<<<<
—Woppler the Weatherman (11:57:21/6-1-52)

>>>>>[Yep. Drek.]<<<<<
—Technocrat (23:35:20/6-3-52)

ACCESS

Plane

Most North American carriers schedule regular flights into the major international airports at Juneau, Anchorage, and Fairbanks. Local carriers such as Northern Lights Airways and Northern Air link smaller cities such as Kodiak, Whitehorse, and Sitka with the international airports. These commuter flights can only operate on a sporadic, weather-dependent schedule during the winter months because of storm activity.

Automobile or Bus

The major land routes into the Athabascan Council lands are Route 37, leading north from Terrace and Kitimat, and Route 97 (the old Alaska Highway) from Fort St. John. Both roads meet at Watson Lake. The only other major road is Route 5, leading south from Inuvik in the Trans-Polar Aleut Nation. During the summer, Whippet Bus Lines and Denali Transport run regular bus service from Fort St. John, Dawson Creek, and Prince Rupert to Whitehorse and points northwest. No major road connects with Juneau, and so travelers wishing to visit this city should consider using air or sea transport.

Sea

Back in the late 20th century, a lucrative cruise ship business sprang up, ferrying tourists up the west coast at a leisurely pace from Vancouver and Prince Rupert to sail along the picturesque Alaskan coastline. Cruises have lost popularity due to the large population of Awakened creatures in the Pacific, but the routes are still traveled, only now by fast ships. The summer ferries sail from Vancouver to Prince Rupert in Tsimshian, and then up the Inside Passage to Juneau, Skagway, Kodiak, and Kenai. During the winter months, only the Prince Rupert to Juneau run is open. The Athabascan Tourist Board advertises the safety of these tours with complete confidence: potential travelers should not take the armored appearance of the ferries as an indication that the runs are dangerous.

>>>>>["Not dangerous" my rosy red rectifier. What about that ferry that got taken down by a fragging kraken two years back?]<<<<<
—Matrix Samurai (18:43:40/8-13-52)

>>>>>[Alternatives to the sea route have been suggested. Some time ago there was talk of paralleling the Athabascan oil pipeline with an evacuated-tunnel maglev link (because they already had the tunnel cut for the aborted second pipeline). Anyone know what happened to that?]<<<<<
—Tuck (5:50:40/10-21-52)

>>>>>[They did a load projection, and canned the project because there'd be frag-all traffic.]<<<<<
—Hardy (17:19:00/10-28-52)

>>>>>[I heard it was 'cause something down there took exception to the presence of the construction assessment crews. That's what I heard.]<<<<<
—Tool Pusher (09:12:13/10-29-52)

TRIBAL DEMOGRAPHICS

The major tribes in the Athabascan Council territories are Aleut and Inuit, with only a few minor tribes making up the balance of the tribally aligned population.

Aleut	35%
Inuit	25%
Koyukon	15%
Yellowknife	10%
Chilcotin	10%
Dene	5%

The vast majority, almost 97 percent, of the population is tribally affiliated. The few non-natives form a single pinkskin tribe based near Anchorage. They hold no significant power in either the government or the business realm, even though they were native to the area when the Council formed. The Athabascan Council gave non-tribal residents the option to stay as citizens, or leave with a small government "relocation assistance" payment when the nation was formed. The vast majority of non-Amerindians left, and the nation immediately faced a significant population problem. The Council sponsors on-going efforts to attract new citizens.

Governmental offices are filled mainly by members of the Athabascan and Aleut tribes. Few Inuit show interest in the positions of power government and the business world provide.

>>>>>[But those who do make one slot of a good showing, especially in business. The CEO of Northern Light Plastics is Inuit, a suit named Norman Fisher (he changed his name to make himself more "acceptable" to Anglo colleagues, I hear). He also sits on the board of Athabascan Oil.]<<<<<
—Ishmael (19:54:50/3-26-52)

Generally speaking, the Inuit population of the Athabascan Council was less willing to adapt to the pace and complexity of contemporary life. The way of life in some fishing villages, particularly along the Aleutian Peninsula, seems little changed from centuries ago. The Athabascans and Aleuts made a smoother transition.

>>>>>[Dangerous generalization, Danchekker, old chummer. Even the most hardcore traditionalist villagers use snowmobiles instead of huskies, and have an electric generator of some kind. Sure, some Inuit still hunt whales in small vessels, but they use Zodiacs or even GEVs, rather than seal-skin coracles.]<<<<<
—Talia (11:25:47/2-28-52)

>>>>>[Talia's right. If you're looking for *really* traditional Inuit culture, look to the northeast, into the Trans-Polar Aleut regions. In the west, they've incorporated the influences of the cultures of Russia and the nations to the south.]<<<<<
—Holly (18:32:10/3-2-52)

HISTORY AND CULTURE

Before the arrival of the European settlers, the far northern region of North America was the most thinly populated area on the continent. The Amerindian tribes that inhabited the western portion of this region belonged in large part to the Athabascan language group. Natives of this area pursued a nomadic, hunting-and-gathering lifestyle that had remained unchanged for centuries because the growing season was generally too short for farming. The Aleut and Inuit concentrated on fishing and hunting whales and seals.

Small bands, each living within its own territory but interrelated by marriage, formed tribes, though there were few tribal chiefs.

The European settlers' arrival had its usual effect on the Athabascan tribes, who entered into trading relationships with the settlers, bartering animal pelts for food, weapons, and equipment. The Inuit and Aleut tribes, however, accepted fewer of the Europeans' ways, preferring their traditional lifestyle.

>>>>>[The Inuit and Aleut probably maintained more of their spiritual traditions than did other Amerindian tribes. They were able to do so because Inuit villages were located in poor trapping areas, and so the settlers mostly ignored them. They headed into the Inuit lands mainly to erect oil rigs, weather stations, and Distant Early Warning radar emplacements. The Inuit responded to these intrusions with characteristic indifference: they simply moved their villages further down the coast, and kept to the old ways. They adopted technology slowly, and even now use only those advances, such as electric generators and snowmobiles, that make life a little easier.]<<<<<
—Holly (09:57:08/10-9-52)

>>>>>[The European influence had another effect, Holly, which was sugar addiction. I go into a lot more detail on this in the Trans-Polar Aleut file; see my entry of 7-21. The Athabascan Council doesn't have it as bad as the T-PA, but it's still an issue.]<<<<<
—People Watcher (05:47:32/10-18-52)

The Dene tribe was the first from this region to join the newly founded SAIM, followed closely by the Koyukon, Yellowknife, and Chilcotin, and several others. These tribes, most notably the Dene, had been at the forefront of the initial land claims made in the late 1990s and early 2000s. The Canadian government generally settled these early claims by paying off the tribes in cash, because it was politically inexpedient to actually give the land back. This solution satisfied those making the land claims for a while, but some militant factions decided that the money was not enough. These factions demanded that the traditional lands be returned to them. They made several attempts to blockade roads and rail lines, but after seeing the fate of the Mohawks in Québec and the Mount Currie band in British Columbia, they abandoned the blockades as soon as they sensed that the government's next response would be through military force.

The Dene tribe's land claims helped establish the Athabascan Council, but the Dene tribe soon withdrew almost completely from government.

>>>>>[Though the back-to-the-land movement is as strong here as anywhere, very few people take wearing traditional garb to heart. After all, a high-tech Gortex parka with R3000 filling is warmer than a sealskin coat any day of the week.]<<<<<
—People Watcher (13:37:17/9-30-52)

>>>>>[But you *do* see a fair number of people with traditional Inuit facial tattooing.]<<<<<
—Holly (20:48:30/10-2-52)

>>>>>[Facial tattooing is very common among go-gangers. You get some pretty extreme stuff—damn near facial mutilation, in some cases.]<<<<<
—SPD (16:58:56/12-27-52)

A TRIBE IN PERSPECTIVE: THE DENE

The Dene tribe (their name is pronounced "Dennay" and is an ancient word meaning "people") is located in what was called the Mackenzie District of the Northwest Territories. The district followed the course of the Mackenzie River and included both the Great Bear and Great Slave lakes. Before the arrival of the European settlers, the Dene shared the hunter-gatherer lifestyle of the other tribes in the Athabascan region. When the Hudson's Bay Company and other

organizations moved into western Canada, the Dene turned more and more to trapping and trading, though they never completely gave up hunting caribou. Even today, caribou meat serves as a vital supplement to the Dene diet. Community organized hunts in both spring and summer range over hundreds of kilometers of the barren-ground regions of the Dene territory.

>>>>>[These hunts are perhaps the single surviving traditional activity and cultural expression of the Dene. They're not just hunts, they're celebrations of the old way of life.]<<<<<
—Holly (00:56:35/2-24-52)

The Dene also continue to hunt beaver, muskrat, and moose. (Modern firearms make hunting this last target considerably safer than it was a century ago.)

>>>>>[No fragging kidding!]<<<<<
—Boomer (00:24:08/3-16-52)

>>>>>[Don't be too sure. Normal moose, yah, sure. But once in a while you run into a snow moose, and things are no longer quite so easy. You know what a snow moose is? I'll put it in words of one syllable: twice as tall as a man, big as a house, mean as a cage of rats. (For more information, check out Paterson's *Paranormal Animals of North America*; it's on the net.)]<<<<<
—Moves Softly (22:53:47/12-2-52)

At first, the European settlers and the Dene coexisted peacefully. The region lacked accessible resources, and the land was too inhospitable for most settlers to covet it for homesteads. This changed in the early 1970s. Canadian utility companies began building hydroelectric dams in the region to produce power, flooding wilderness valleys and encroaching on the hunting grounds—and often the homes—of native tribes, including the Dene. The Dene and another group, the Metis, began petitioning the Canadian government to prevent further depredations, following up with official land claims.

Things became even more interesting when two companies proposed to run natural gas pipelines up the Mackenzie River valley, directly through the heart of the territory claimed by the Dene. The Dene objected, and proposed that the Canadian government block any pipeline construction until the Dene land claim was settled. In 1976, the Canadian government and the Dene agreed, in principle, to this plan of action.

The agreement did not hold up. The pipeline was built long before 1999, when the Dene land claim was eventually disallowed. The rights and wishes of the Dene people were disregarded.

>>>>>[I was there, and I saw. I was young, but I remember my people blocking the bulldozers with their bodies. I saw the soldiers come, and my people fighting them and killing them. And the helicopters came and shot my people down like mad dogs.]<<<<<
—T'Seleie (18:34:42/12-13-52)

The corporations forced a similar pipeline through a neighboring territory claimed by the Metis. The Metis did not risk violent confrontation by blocking construction. They simply waited for the pipeline to be completed and then sabotaged it. The Canadian government sent in the newly expanded CSIS security and intelligence forces to arrest the perpetrators, but the entire Metis tribe opposed this force, and so no individuals could be singled out. The government's invasion sparked the Second Metis Rebellion, which led to the virtual extinction of that tribe.

The Dene learned their lesson. Instead of sabotage, they used political and propaganda campaigns to fight the Canadian government. When SAIM formed, the Dene tribe was first in line to take advantage of their larger political clout.

Initially, as the tentative boundaries of the NAN nations were formed, it looked as though the land that is now the Athabascan Council would go to the Algonkian-Manitoo Council. The Dene people fought this division, forcing the NAN to declare the Athabascan Council a distinct state.

Things did not work out quite as the Dene had planned, however. They forced the NAN to establish the Athabascan Council separate from the Algonkian-Manitoo Council, planning to split away and create a sovereign Dene Nation. But the Athabascan Council blocked them. They succeeded in avoiding the shackles of one oppressor, only to find themselves ruled by another government, ruled without a voice. The Dene are an unhappy people.

>>>>>[Oh, you're so poetic, Danchekker, you slot. No, the Dene are not happy with the way things have turned out. But we'll fix that, don't you worry. We're patient.]<<<<<
—Amen (07:57:50/12-19-52)

ECONOMY

The Athabascan Council economy is almost exclusively resource-based. Though the demand for petroleum as a fuel has dropped by a factor of ten over the past half-century, the plastics industry still needs oil and oil by-products. (In the next ten years this too will change, as the silicon-based polymer "pseudo-plastics" become more sophisticated and cheaper. For the moment, however, petrochemicals still form the cornerstone of the plastics industry.)

In the middle of the 20th century, several parties recognized the significance and value of the vast Athabascan Tar Sands. Over the next 50 years, these companies drew off most of the easily extracted oil, and the Tar Sands were abandoned in 2001 as no longer economically feasible. In 2011 Biogene Laboratories Inc. marketed the first efficient oil-leeching bacteria and the Tar Sands were once more an economic boon.

The bacteria leech oil from the Sands, then the oil must be recovered from the bacteria. This process takes place in large extraction plants based in the new industrial town of Xenium.

>>>>>[For those who would like to know, "Xenium" is Greek for "gift" (which is what the Tar Sands project must seem like to the Athabascans).]<<<<<
—Daon (9:05:32/9-12-52)

>>>>>[And Xenium is really an industrial hell-hole of a town. You've got to see it (and smell it) to believe it.]<<<<<
—Tool Pusher (22:12:41/9-14-52)

After the oil is extracted from the bacteria, it is transferred via pipeline to refinery facilities in and around Anchorage. The Tar Sands crude is mixed with crude drawn from depleted oil patches in the northern Athabascan Council region. Most of this mixture goes south by pipeline to the Salish-Shidhe Council and California Free State. The rest is loaded aboard robot tankers in Kodiak Harbor and shipped elsewhere around the Pacific Rim.

Apart from oil-related industry, the Athabascan Council has very little in the way of high technology.

>>>>>[Want to hear something real scary? The Athabascans don't own the oil-leeching bacteria. They license the right to use the biotech on a year-by-year basis from the developers, Biogene Laboratories Inc. And who recently purchased Biogene, lock, stock, and gas chromatograph? Yakashima Technologies, a Japanese biotech concern. They take a keen interest in bioengineering, but they've successfully kept a low profile, so not many people even know about them. I suspect, however, that we'll be hearing more about Yakashima and Biogene in the next few years.]<<<<<
—Overseer (05:33:58/4-28-52)

The two largest locally owned corporations are Athabascan Oil and Northern Light Plastics.

>>>>>[Both are owned indirectly by the same holding company, but good luck trying to prove it. The pay-data's buried unbelievably deep. I had to hire a real top gun to dig up even this one fact.]<<<<<
—Pascal (07:34:52/4-6-52)

>>>>>[Thanks for the testimonial.]<<<<<
—FastJack (16:20:48/4-8-52)

>>>>>[Here's the good stuff: price differentials with respect to Seattle. Enjoy!

ATHABASCAN COST OF LIVING

ITEM	COST
Weaponry	
Ammunition	100% (1)*
Explosives	90% (2)
Firearm Accessories	110%
Firearms	110%
Melee Weapons	90%
Projectile Weapons	95%
Throwing Weapons	80%
Armor and Clothing	
Armor	110% (3)
Security and Surveillance	
Communications	110%
Security Devices	130% (4)
Surveillance Countermeasures	130%
Surveillance Measures	130%
Survival Gear	60%
Vision Enhancers	120%
Lifestyle	
Lifestyle	80%
Electronics	
Electronics	110%
Cybertech	
Biotech	110%
Bodyware	150%
Cyberdecks	290% (7)
Headware	150% (5)
Internals	150% (6)
Programs	150%+ (8)
Magical Equipment	
Hermetic Library	150%+
Magical Supplies	90%
Magical Weapons	160%
Power Foci	80%
Ritual Sorcery Materials	20%
Spell Foci	80%
Vehicles	
Aircraft	180%
Boats	130%
Ground Vehicles	150%
Military Vehicles	100% (9)

*Cost of Living Notes

(1) You can track down belt-fed ordnance here, but not explosive stuff and military grade rounds (i.e., cannon shells and APDS rounds). (Shadow channels excepted, of course.)

(2) Explosives are used for a drek-load of legitimate purposes in this area, making them easier to get than in other places.

Permits are still officially required, but any runner worth his salt can find a mechanic to fake up as much paper as he needs. Be warned, though: by law, all explosives must have a chemical trace compound that identifies the batch and the source. This chemical trace can be picked up from the residue of an explosion. You might be able to track down "clean" explosives through shadow channels, but the price is going to be nearly double. Possession of clean explosives is a major no-no in the eyes of the law.

(3) Light body armor only. Security-grade and military armor is highly restricted...officially. I happen to know that a few sec-guards at Athabascan Oil supplement their income by selling anything that isn't tied down, accounting for it as "storm damage."

(4) Same situation as armor: see the boys at AthOil.

(5) Hard to get, and check the references of your body shop real carefully.

(6) Ditto headware.

(7) None manufactured locally (officially), and import is strictly illegal. However, a couple of people in Anchorage build decks to personal spec. Takes time and costs nuyen, of course, but in the long run it's better than buying off the shelf.

(8) Same as cyberdecks. Write your own, or go see one of the two or three competent people in Anchorage.

(9) This multiplier means that you're going to have to pay a fixer the same outrageous commission you would in Seattle. Demand and supply are both low, so you might be able to bargain. (I know one guy who picked up a storm-damaged Citymaster from the kind folks at AthOil—god knows why he wanted one. It set him back a cool 3 million nuyen.)]<<<<<
—The Keynesian Kid*(17:06:45/2-11-52)

>>>>>[The Kid didn't mention alcohol or chips. Prices for everything mind-altering are low, maybe 75 percent of what you'd pay anywhere else. The reason? Market conditions, chummer. Just about *everyone* abuses something, particularly in the smaller settlements and in the middle of winter. Mainly because there's drek-all else to do. The mind-benders of choice are BTL chips and that good old standby ethyl alcohol, flavored to taste.]<<<<<
—Warpdrive (15:13:57/2-27-52)

>>>>>[AthOil has seen some nasty incidents recently, when tool pushers and even supervisors got crammed out of their pointy little skulls while on-shift.]<<<<<
—Sally Steel (13:48:42/7-13-52)

>>>>>[Gangs are starting to be a real problem in Athabasca, for the same reasons the residents chip out: sheer boredom. Thriller gangs cover the cities, and ersatz go-gangs terrorize the smaller towns. The go-gangs adapt to the conditions, of course. In the winter, they don't use bikes, they use snowmobiles and customized Hovercats, with weapons fixed on hardpoints or firmpoints. At the moment, the hot ganger list includes Aurora, Frostfire, the Wind Chillers, and the Nomads. These guys are hard on the locals, and they're real bad news if you look like you don't belong.]<<<<<
—Yoshi (17:10:18/7-21-52)

>>>>>[And most of them are blasted out of their minds.]<<<<<
—JoJo (08:07:36/7-25-52)

>>>>>[The government and the cops take a stab at coming down hard on the BTL trade, but get very few results. Most of the real choice junk comes up from the Sioux Nation.]<<<<<
—SPD (00:59:13/7-31-52)

Feeding the Athabascan nation has always been a problem. The Council is wealthy, particularly when compared to the other northern nations, but must spend the lion's share of its oil revenues to import food. The Council hoped to become more self-sufficient by creating huge hydroponic and greenhouse projects to grow food using solar and locally generated nuclear power. Unfortunately, storm damage decreased yields and increased maintenance costs to the point where the projects are only marginally more cost-efficient than the original import system.

>>>>>[Danchekker follows the party line, as always. The problems here resemble AthOil's storm damage, but are more serious. "Storm damage" doesn't scramble optical chips in shielded CPUs running fusion reactors buried under 20 meters of permafrost. It doesn't fill security guards full of flechettes, or splice innocuous data into surveillance systems to cover up what's really going down. We're talking sabotage here, chummers. I don't know who's doing it, but I know it's being done.]<<<<<
—Harley (10:58:39/4-10-52)

>>>>>[The first question to ask is always, "Who benefits?" Or, rather, "Who suffers if inexpensive, locally grown food becomes available?" At first glance, I'd say the major exporters to Athabasca, the S-S Council and Sioux, right?]<<<<<
—Nuyen Nick (23:01:29/4-20-52)

>>>>>[Or the company shipping the majority of food into Athabasca, Free Transit Cartage.]<<<<<
—Jammer (09:06:02/4-21-52)

>>>>>[And Free Transit just happens to be owned by...care to venture a guess?]<<<<<
—Pyramid Watcher (06:03:27/4-27-52)

>>>>>[Don't forget, there's also a good number of anti-tech groups that just don't like the idea of nuclear power. These guys might decide to kill people to prove that the technology could kill people. (Hey—that argument's been around for a long time, and it's never made sense.)]<<<<<
—Random (13:28:38/4-30-52)

>>>>>[The Council's branching off into another area that's stirring up a drek-load of controversy. You've heard about fish farming, right? Well, how about whale farming? The Council's raising a herd of humpbacks that they plan to "harvest" in five years. Lots of protein and no problems with storms like you get with hydroponic farms. And the "herd" is easy to train. Makes lots of sense, huh? Well, frag, the whole idea's got enough eco-freaks jumping up and down to shake the entire west coast into the sea. Slot it, chummer, it's whales, okay? I thought we settled this whole issue at the end of the century.]<<<<<
—Dr. Spike (11:21:50/7-7-52)

>>>>>[Dr. Spike is correct. The issue was settled last century, with regard to whales that are considered intelligent, or capable of becoming intelligent in a time frame less than the geologic. We at Farm-the-Sea Inc. are as horrified as anyone at the thought of harvesting a sentient creature, or one truly on its way to sentience. I think all reasonable people will agree that this parameter does not apply to traditional food animals, such as cows. And our research has proven beyond a shadow of a doubt that the sentience parameter does not apply to gray whales. (You will note that I limit my comments to that species alone. I agree that sperm whales and blue whales, among others, show rudiments of intelligence. This is why Farm-the-Sea Inc. is not planning to reduce these species to consumable protein.) We at Farm-the-Sea strongly believe that world hunger is the major hindrance to the further development of the human and metahuman species. It is our goal to eliminate world hunger by 2075 through the development of new and innovative protein sources, such as our whale-farming program.]<<<<<
—Hollis Baynes, CEO, Farm-the-Sea Inc. (13:48:20/7-9-52)

>>>>>[Fragging apologist.]<<<<<
—Shogun (14:12:39/7-9-52)

>>>>>[Anybody interested in reducing Hollis Baynes to consumable protein should contact me at LTG# 1907 (76-0683).]<<<<<
—Deerhunter (23:48:52/7-21-52)

GOVERNMENT

The Athabascan Council government operates under the democratic system of an executive branch and a bicameral house. The supreme executive is the governor of the Grand Council and is named by open election every five years. The bicameral house consists of the Upper and Lower Councils. The Upper Council is elected by general ballot. All candidates' names appear on the ballot, and the 50 candidates receiving the most votes comprise the Upper Council. One hundred distinct electoral districts vote to fill the Lower Council. These electoral districts originally corresponded to sub-tribal groups and communities, but the system has failed to keep up with shifts in population. Upper and Lower Council members serve four-year terms, with the elections offset by two years.

The Grand Council, of which the governor is nominally the chairman, comprises the ten members of the governor's cabinet and ten independent representatives. The Upper and Lower Councils select the independent representatives according to a complex process. The independent representatives serve the same term as the governor.

>>>>>[The current Governor is a Bear shaman who calls herself Mary Windwalker (translated from the Inuktituk, I understand). Good administrator, but lacks vision.]<<<<<
—Yobbo (05:38:21/8-8-52)

>>>>>[I once had the singular honor of bugging a combined Council election session. They were trying to choose representatives to the Grand Council. As someone who's been around the political block several times, I didn't think I could be surprised. I was wrong. The amount of backstabbing, influence-peddling, and horse trading that I heard was staggering. UCAS representatives should think twice before sitting down across the table from these folks. It would be like the lion lying down with the lamb: only one is going to get up again.]<<<<<
—Alfred Evenstar (10:41:57/9-12-52)

>>>>>[The unofficial spokesman of the Upper Council is another member of the Windwalker clan, Mary's cousin Billy. The story I hear is that he used to run with a hardcore thriller gang called the Nomads, and he used to be a drek-hot hermetic mage. When he burned out, he got himself some chrome and then somehow found his way into politics. Weird guy: people respect him in the abstract, but fear him personally.]<<<<<
—A.B. (21:19:47/10-5-52)

LAWS

IMMIGRATION

The Council's population suffered a significant, near-catastrophic slump immediately after the nation formed. A large segment of the more highly educated and highly trained members of society emigrated to greener pastures, fearing the loss of their lifestyle. This population slump reversed itself over the years immediately following, as other tribally affiliated intelligentsia immigrated to Athabasca. Over the last three years, however, the population has started to decline once more, the majority again being lost from the well-educated sector of society.

In an attempt to reverse this new "brain drain," the Council instituted a "bounty" system. Bounty payments are assigned to a wide variety of trades and professions. Anyone applying for citizenship who qualifies in a "bounty profession" receives a lump-sum payment ranging from 5,000¥ for low-level programmers to well over 100,000¥ for chimeric gene-splicers. Citizenship is open to virtually all applicants, regardless of race, education, or profession. A criminal record does not automatically disqualify an applicant, although the government shies away from extending welcome to convicted mass-murderers or other obvious undesirables. Work visas do not exist because only citizens can be officially employed. This serves as an obvious incentive to prospective immigrants.

>>>>>[Unlike the requirements for citizenship in some other nations, when you apply for Athabascan citizenship you may retain other citizenships you hold. It's a shameless come-on: you've got nothing to lose.]<<<<<
—Tandy (14:04:23/6-12-52)

>>>>>[The Council tends to play fast and loose with its citizenship lists. I know for a fact that more than 10,000 dead people are still listed as citizens-in-good-standing. Why, pray tell?]<<<<<
—Prester John (07:02:58/6-30-52)

>>>>>[Probably some kind of political scam they're working on the NAN. Aren't some votes weighted by national population? If so, then the "brain drain" is also leeching away Athabasca's clout in the Sovereign Council.]<<<<<
—Golden Bear (10:14:24/7-4-52)

>>>>>[You got it, chummer.]<<<<<
—Willard (21:09:11/7-10-52)

CIVIL AND TRIBAL LAWS

The Council's justice system is built around one hundred small judiciary regions that correspond to the electoral districts. Cases are heard by a local judiciary council. Cases involving jurisdiction disputes (for example, if a fugitive crosses a district boundary), are decided by a combined council of the judiciary councils of each district claiming jurisdiction.

The Athabascan Council legal system resembles the Napoleonic code used in Québec. No prosecutors or defense attorneys are used, and the judge participates in uncovering the truth rather than functioning as an objective observer. No distinction is made between civil and criminal law. Except in capital cases, where the judiciary council's decision must be ratified by the Lower Council of the national government, no provision exists for appeal. The local council's decision is binding.

>>>>>[Because they don't like giving up their authority to the national government, very few local councils impose the death sentence. They just chuck the poor sod away for a kabillion years with a chance of parole after a century or two. Apart from that, sentences and fines are what you'd expect to receive in Seattle.]<<<<<
—Legal Beagle (14:20:01/7-2-52)

>>>>>[Gun laws are very strictly worded but rarely enforced. Officially, only hunting weapons may be legally owned by a private party, but it seems that Athabascans like a good deal of firepower when they go hunting. Belt-fed, explosive, and APDS ammo is not cool, but most cops will turn a blind eye to smartguns (as long as the cops are confident that they can out-gun you in a pinch, that is). The gun laws are only strictly enforced at the border, so don't try to bring your trusty Uzi across. Stick to hunting rifles and pick up the wiz stuff once you're inside.]<<<<<
—Tommyknocker (11:01:24/7-3-52)

INTERNATIONAL RELATIONS

The Athabascan Council honors free-trade pacts with its immediate neighbors. These pacts eliminate all tariffs and duties and open up the borders of the Council for import and export. Trade restrictions still exist, of course. Free trade or not, importing explosives, military weapons, and restricted security equipment without an authorization certificate is illegal.

>>>>>[Which any kid with a Sony-Apple ColorPress™ system can knock off for you in five minutes.]<<<<<
—Hangfire (15:14:09/3-10-52)

It is also illegal to export items made of natural walrus ivory, and artwork of authentic Inuit origin.

The Athabascan Council enjoys close ties with the Salish-Shidhe Council and the Trans-Polar Aleut Nation. Relations are cool with Tsimshian, and currently somewhat strained with the Algonkian-Manitoo Council.

>>>>>[Turf wars. See my entry on the A-M Council.]<<<<<
—Lounge Lizard (21:43:02/5-22-52)

>>>>>[Daniel Iniuk reps Athabasca on the NAN Sovereign Council. Straight suit is the way I read him: mundane, and no chrome. A touch bent in the head.]<<<<<
—Wally (07:22:17/5-27-52)

>>>>>[Not quite a straight suit. He's got so much headware that his processing horsepower rivals a NeoVAX. I think that's why he's "a touch bent in the head."]<<<<<
—Amber (15:24:53/6-3-52)

>>>>>[Iniuk dropped out of sight after the NAN ruled against him in the A-M land dispute. "Well-deserved vacation" is how the press releases read, but the dirt on the street is that he's emotionally crashed. Some people say he won't be back.]<<<<<
—Matrix Marauder (02:01:03/6-12-52)

GENERAL COMMENTS

The Athabascan standard of living is slightly lower than in the Algonkian-Manitoo Council, but the government's coffers are considerably fuller. This state of affairs allows the Council to offer a range of health and welfare services that is the envy of many North American nations. The government subsidizes a universal health insurance, and the welfare and unemployment insurance programs are well-funded.

>>>>>[Sorry, Danchekker, old chummer. BUZZ—thanks for playing! Health insurance, welfare, and unemployment are universally available, but they're *not* well-funded. In fact, the government only keeps them going through internal borrowing against better-run programs. These three social programs aren't self-supporting, and it's just a matter of time until they go bankrupt.]<<<<<
—The Keynesian Kid (15:33:23/7-9-52)

>>>>>[We're starting to see the results of this internal borrowing in the medical system. A few years back, the government created "user fees" for the health insurance program. Since then, the user fees have skyrocketed almost to what you'd pay in Seattle if you didn't have any health insurance at all. But people still have to kick into the medical services plan through their taxes. The government won't allow private insurers into the market, because that would be a tacit admission that their own program is going belly-up. An increasing number of Athabascan citizens pay into UCAS-based health plans and come to Seattle for treatment. That tells you something.]<<<<<
—Doc U-Dub (19:09:01/7-11-52)

The Athabascan Council continues to insist, according to its 2035 decision, that the UCAS remove all DEW sensor stations from Athabascan lands.

>>>>>[The stations aren't gone yet, are they, Danchekker? Understandably, the UCAS military didn't feel too warm-and-fuzzy when the Council told them to pick up their toys and go home. At first, the UCAS played macho: "Oh, yeah? Make me." Athabasca was stumped. Standing up to the UCAS military was just an efficient form of suicide, and they knew it. Their only chance was to infiltrate and blow all the stations at once, and hope that the UCAS would decide revenge wasn't worth the tab. The DEW emplacements were under-defended, and so the raid was feasible. UCAS recognized the same possibility, of course. Before the Athabascans could go in with their plastique, UCAS folded. "Okay, boys, we'll pull out," is what they said, "but it'll take us some time." They haven't done much since, but, significantly, they haven't reinforced the defence of their stations. It's obvious that neither side wants to provoke the other. Interesting gavotte.]<<<<<
—Sun Tzu II (05:05:03/11-11-52)

>>>>>[Here's the basis for the Council's discomfort. The UCAS—and the white man in general—has thermonukes and delivery systems. And now he has magic. The only thing that once set us apart from the white man and helped balance his military superiority is no longer exclusively ours. To (mis)quote an old aphorism, "Walk a mile in our moccasins." You'll understand why we're touchy.]<<<<<
—Prowling Bear (06:42:55/11-21-52)

TRANS-POLAR ALEUT NATION

FACTS AT A GLANCE

Population: 6,385,000
    Human: 80%
    Elf: 2%
    Dwarf: 2%
    Ork: 11%
    Troll: 4%
    Other: 1%
Per Capita Income: 3,500¥
Population Below Poverty Level: 87%
On Fortune's Active Traders List: 0%
Corporate Affiliation: 1%
Education:
    High School Equivalency: 51%
    College Equivalency: 12%
    Advanced Studies Certificates: 2%
Regional Telecom Grid Access: NA/TPA

CLIMATE

The Trans-Polar Aleut Nation covers the northernmost regions of what were once Alaska, the Yukon, and the Northwest Territories of North America, the northern areas of the eastern Soviet Union, and the entirety of Greenland and Iceland. The nation also includes several million hectares of more-or-less permanent ice cap. (The annual fluctuations of the ice cap make the Trans-Polar Aleut Nation the only sovereign country whose total land-mass varies by more than 10 percent from summer to winter.)

In the southernmost regions, summer temperatures climb to only around 20 degrees Celsius. In the majority of the nation, however, summertime temperatures rarely reach 0° C. The wind chill can push temperatures as low as –100° C in winter. These harsh conditions allow the Trans-Polar Aleut Nation little to no tourism industry.

>>>>>[Fragging-A, chummer. Save your nuyen, and visit your local meat packer's walk-in freezer. The effect's just the same.]<<<<<
    —Fisher (19:05:27/1-14-52)

>>>>>[I know I'm coming across as bug-paranoid, but watch out for pseudo-VITAS-carrying mosquitos in the south in summer. Two deaths so far this year. I'm not kidding.]<<<<<
    —Dan the Man (19:30:13/6-19-52)

The entire Trans-Polar Aleut Nation lies within the Arctic Circle, and so the amount of light each day is at extremes throughout the year. For several weeks in mid-summer, the sun never drops completely below the horizon, creating the famous "white nights." In mid-winter, several weeks of continual night wreak havoc on biorhythms and lifestyles.

>>>>>[This phenomenon is the T-PA's one tourist draw. They gain some revenue from touting themselves as the "land of the midnight sun." In June and July, enterprising tour companies ship jaded looky-loos up to Inuvik to gaze in awe and wonder at the midnight sun. Then they ship them back to their comfortable homes. Vultures.]<<<<<
    —Aurora (04:50:43/6-28-52)

>>>>>[I understand your cynicism, Aurora. But you can't deny the impact of the white nights. The midnight sun has profound psychological effects on residents and tourists alike. Doesn't your own diurnal rhythm change? (I notice your entry is time-stamped 4:50 A.M. near mid-summer. Are you up and around *and lucid* before 5 A.M. in December?) Isn't it true that there's a sort of nervous, frenetic feel to everything when the sun doesn't set? Aren't there more bar brawls and murders in June and July than December and January? And doesn't the suicide count spike around mid-winter?]<<<<<
    —Goose (22:54:11/7-1-52)

>>>>>[Point taken. You sound like you know what you're talking about, Goose.]<<<<<
    —Aurora (01:22:13/7-2-52)

>>>>>[I spent one (very weird and probably not-to-be-repeated) year in Tuktoyaktuk.]<<<<<
    —Goose (06:23:20/7-5-52)

>>>>>[Aurora didn't mention the phenomenon she (probably) named herself after, the aurora borealis. Spectacular as all hell, and worth the hardship of the climate. Once seen, never forgotten, I assure you.]<<<<<
    —Davey (09:02:29/7-28-52)

ACCESS

Plane

Four international airports serve the Trans-Polar Aleut Nation: Inuvik (the capital), Reykjavik (one-time Iceland), Godth b (Greenland), and Nordvik (Soviet Union). Inuvik International is by far the largest of the four, but is still a very small airport compared with any other major terminus in the world. Semi-ballistic traffic is not available at any of these airports, but all boast a regular schedule of suborbital arrivals and departures.

>>>>>[Regular, sure. Every second week, whether any seats have been sold or not.]<<<<<
—Wingz (12:52:20/ 10-21-52)

>>>>>[Come on, chummer, it ain't quite that bad. The Inuvik–Seattle hop runs Mondays and Thursdays, and Reykjavik–New York goes Tuesdays and Fridays. As you'd expect, charter companies and plane rental outfits do a good trade in flying minor corporate execs who don't have their own birds but just *have* to be in T-PA by tomorrow morning.]<<<<<
—Midnight Rocker (10:07:36/11-7-52)

A number of locally owned short-haul carriers handle connections between the main hub cities and other destinations in Trans-Polar Aleut.

>>>>>[The only local carrier worth considering is Trans-Polar Air. It does twice the business of all the other carriers combined, and has on-time and safety records an order of magnitude better than its closest competitor. Of course, there's a downside (but there always is, right, chummer?). The planes are old Super-Twin Otters—that's right, the design is 25 years old. Reliable as hell, but as comfortable as a dump truck with one square wheel. The rigger controls are pretty new, which is a bonus, and the fly-boys are some of the best in the biz.]<<<<<
—Sky Pilot (01:48:38/8-14-52)

>>>>>[You didn't mention the company you fly for, Sky Pilot. What is it, Trans-Polar Air? Thought so.]<<<<<
—Bongo (06:24:56/12-9-52)

Automobile or Bus

Inuvik is the only large city in the Trans-Polar Aleut Nation accessible via a major highway, Route 5 north from Dawson (not Dawson Creek) in the Athabascan Council. Despite the use of subsurface heaters and regular plowing, even this road is often impassable in winter. Nation-wide, general terrain conditions and the widespread lack of roads make wheeled transport impractical for most of the year.

Whippet Bus Lines runs semi-weekly service from Dawson to Inuvik June through August.

Alternative Transport

Low Altitude Vehicle (LAV) and Ground Effect Vehicle (GEV) service supplements short-haul air carriers for providing internal transportation. These services also extend across the borders and offer another route into the country.

>>>>>[In other words, you can hop a T-bird from Hebron (Québec) to Frobisher Bay (T-PA), or Yellowknife (Athabascan) to Cambridge Bay (T-PA). They're not real T-birds—no armor or weapons, or firm/hardpoints to mount anything—but they're LAVs just the same. I suspect a lot of the riggers are ex-military. LAV/GEV service probably goes to other parts of the T-PA too, but I'm not aware of it.]<<<<<
—King Crimson (15:26:05/3-26-52)

TRIBAL DEMOGRAPHICS

The two major tribes in the Trans-Polar Aleut Nation are Aleut and Inuit. The population breaks down 75–25 percent in favor of the Inuit, even though the Aleut have a far greater presence in government and business. As in the Athabascan Council, the Inuit population has adapted less fully—or less willingly—to the changing face of contemporary life. Many fishing villages appear to maintain the lifestyle they have lived for centuries. This is particularly true in Baffin Island, Greenland, and Iceland. In the region around Inuvik and directly north, Banks, Victoria, and Melville islands, the proximity of the Athabascan Council appears to have forced the inhabitants back into a 1950s lifestyle. The Aleuts generally have made a smoother transition.

When the Trans-Polar Aleut Nation formed, it expelled practically all non-native residents. In the intervening years, however, the country bowed to the inevitable and allowed a limited number of non-natives, particularly those with needed skill-sets, back into the territory. The proportion of non-natives is still less than 2 percent of the total population. These immigrants find acceptance and respect professionally, but personally find themselves outsiders. Non-natives generally restrict themselves to restaurants, bars, and other establishments associated with the companies employing them, because they are not welcome elsewhere. No "pinkskin tribes" make their home within the nation.

>>>>>[Danchekker's got that right. I'm Anglo, and came to work for Bathotech in Inuvik in 2047. I thought it would be a friendly gesture to get to know my neighbors, so I visited a downtown watering hole called The Ice Blink. At first I was just ignored, which was bad enough. Then a couple of young toughs, blasted out of their minds, decided it would be fun to mess with the Anglo. When I caught their drift, I tried to make a graceful exit, but they weren't having any of that. *They* started the brawl, so I don't feel bad about putting them in the clinic. (Guess they didn't realize that heavy-gear wranglers like me often have muscle boosts.) Anyhow, that was the first and last time I ever tried to have a drink anywhere outside the Bathotech enclave.]<<<<<
—Tool Pusher (14:04:00/12-14-52)

A large percentage of the native population feels at least some kinship with other nations' "back-to-the-land" movements. Many sub-tribal groups live, by choice, much the way their ancestors did a century ago. Even those who have not fully embraced the old lifestyle have re-adopted the native traditions of personal adornment. In keeping with the old ways, upon reaching puberty, many boys have their lower lips pierced near the corner of the mouth, and many women have their chins tattooed after their first menstruation.

>>>>>[Marriage customs remain highly traditional, too. Arranged marriages are still common, and the prospective groom often lives in the wife's household for the year prior to the marriage, helping the father in his trade. Polygamous marriages are common: one man with two women, or two men with one woman. It's nearly acceptable for a native man to marry a non-native woman as long as he also has another, native wife to "keep the Anglo in line," but the reverse is completely unacceptable. And a native woman even considering a liaison with a non-native man will be ostracized.]<<<<<
—Holly (21:12:35/10-22-52)

HISTORY AND CULTURE

Many tribes of the Trans-Polar Aleut area successfully ignored the arrival of the European settlers until well into the 20th century. They pursued their traditional lifestyles undisturbed by what was happening elsewhere on the continent.

This easy coexistence began to change when the Europeans discovered the rich natural resources of the Far North. Oil exploration and drilling, and later the search for natural gas, and later still the quest for geothermal power, sent companies to the north. Yet even these European incursions failed to dramatically affect the native Amerindians. The area of the Far North was huge, after all, and if a hunter-gatherer band disliked the proximity of the Anglos, it could simply move on, losing nothing in the process.

In the late 1990s and early 2000s, the world scrambled for control of the last remnants of its depleted reserves of fossil fuels. More companies moved north, and the effects on the native tribes became more and more pronounced. Drilling rigs fouled bays and damaged fisheries, and projects based on the ice cap disturbed the migration routes of whales and seals, upon which many bands depended for food.

In the northern areas of the Soviet Union, the condition of the native tribes deteriorated even more rapidly as the government initiated projects that threatened the ecology without any thought as to how a massive imbalance would affect the indigenous peoples. The search for exploitable resources included the creation of oil and gas recovery sites and geothermal energy plants, situated on the continental shelf under the ice cap.

>>>>>[What's wrong with geothermal energy? I thought it was one of the cleanest things going.]<<<<<
—Barnes (11:55:38/10-1-52)

>>>>>[It is, if it's done right. The Sovs just didn't do it right. Think about it: whether it's a geothermal station, a fusion reactor, or a shopping mall, you have to build the thing. And if you're not careful, you'll frag up the environment doing it, right? For example, when you're excavating the primary pit, the right thing to do with the junk you're digging up is to dump it where it won't do any damage and build yourself a nice harmless island or something. The *easiest* thing to do is just spew it out into the water where you're boring, silting up rivers, killing fish, and so on. Any guesses as to which option the Sovs took?]<<<<<
—Ryan (01:07:05/10-16-52)

The advance of civilization was finally starting to encroach on the lifestyle of the area's natives. While elsewhere in the world, native peoples challenged established governments with their new-found political power, the tribes of the Far North found that their isolationist approach to "modern civilization" would now hurt them. They had no unity. They had no political power. All across the North American continent, native bands and tribes applied political pressure significant enough to force admittedly often violent responses from national governments. By contrast, in the Far North before 2010, the largest political unit—if that term can be applied to such a small group—was the individual village. The Aleut and Inuit peoples were backed into a corner, their only options extinction or union with the "invaders."

This situation changed as the level of magical energy, or mana, in the world increased. The Inuit people had almost effortlessly retained many of their old traditions and ceremonies; as magic returned to the world, they found their old ceremonies raising and controlling magical powers that they had believed to be only myths. Shamans discovered that many traditional art forms could be used to petition power from the most common Far North totems, Whale, Seal, Walrus, and Polar Bear. Even though the Inuit, and, to a lesser degree, the Aleut, harnessed magical power, their individualistic, piecemeal society prevented them from organizing enough strength to affect the white man's advances.

The tribes needed unity, and it appeared in the person of a shamanic leader who took the name Ininook. Even today, nobody knows for sure where Ininook came from, but most sources agree he probably emerged from the northern reaches of the Soviet Union. Protected by spirits, he made the long trek across the pole and settled on Cornwallis Island near Resolute.

Ininook spent several years building stable channels of communication between bands who, until this point, had seen no need for such communication. Technology was limited, but magic proved to be much better than radios and telephones. Watcher spirits connected the tribal shamans.

Ininook's whereabouts during all this are a mystery. Some wilder theories claim that the shaman was in fact nowhere on Earth, but hiding on the astral or another plane. Most analysts believe, however, that he was simply traveling around the Far North, using his own undeniable personal magnetism to cement a union between the diverse tribes and bands. Wherever he was, Ininook succeeded in his goal. He forged a consensus among the tribes and applied to SAIM for official membership, which was granted immediately.

For most Far North tribes, membership in SAIM involved mere lip service. They had little input into SAIM's plans, and SAIM had little to offer in return. The symbolic value of SAIM membership was effective, however. As soon as SAIM granted membership to the Trans-Polar Aleut "nation," the vast majority of the remaining Anglos moved out.

>>>>>[No surprises there. We feared—and perhaps rightly so—that we'd be cut off from the rest of what we called civilization, hunted down, and killed. (Remember, pogroms were an ugly reality in some of the other NAN nations.)]<<<<<
—Toby (12:57:28/3-17-52)

Many tribal groups believed that when the Anglos left, the threats against their way of life left too. The alliances that Ininook forged quickly fragmented, and the Trans-Polar Aleut Nation reverted to a very loose federation of disparate elements. Ininook knew that the threat had not vanished; in fact, it had only just begun, but even the force of his personality could not keep the groups together. The general threat to the native way of life was lessened, but resources attractive to other nations existed in Trans-Polar Aleut, and military takeover was a very real possibility.

Ininook was wrong. A military threat never materialized against the Trans-Polar Aleut Nation—the only sovereign Amerindian nation able to make this claim.

>>>>>[To echo Toby, "no surprise there." Military action against a nation must be targeted against a government, a central administration, or organized armed forces. The T-PA had none of these. What the hell were the armed forces of the U.S. and Canada (and later the UCAS) or the Soviet Union to do? Blow the drek out of several hundred fishing villages? Eradicate a couple of thousand migratory bands of seal hunters? It's kind of like attacking a rainstorm by targeting individual raindrops.]<<<<<
—Randall (18:55:02/4-10-52)

>>>>>[Lousy analogy, but it gets the point across.]<<<<<
—People Watcher (06:03:28/4-11-52)

Others eventually accepted the mantle of political leadership. Native leaders established a very loose governmental structure in Inuvik; Ininook faded from the scene, and was never heard from again.

>>>>>[Ininook cared nothing for politics, he cared about his people. Once their survival was assured, he left the work to those with temperaments better suited to maintaining and guiding political control.]<<<<<
—T'lilik (13:08:27/5-5-52)

A TRIBE IN PERSPECTIVE: THE ALEUT

The term "Aleut" was originally applied only to the inhabitants of the Aleutian Islands, an archipelago extending from the mainland of what was once Alaska into the Bering Sea. Over the years, the name has been expanded to include a number of groups sharing a common language. These tribes lived in the area north of the Aleutians toward the North Pole.

The peoples of the Aleut language group lived by hunting and fishing, following the migratory whales and seals that made up the bulk of their diet. Villages of fewer than a dozen families made up their largest organized groups; family bands were much more common. As described in the general discussion above, they had minimal contact with the "white men" when they came to the Arctic regions.

Most Aleut bands maintained a strong religious tradition even in the 20th century, when the level of mana in the world was extremely low. Their ceremonies depended heavily on dances, chants, and songs. In the early 21st century, the shamans discovered that the old magic myths were true. They could command and control the forces of magic through their traditional chants and dances.

Without the efforts of the great shaman Ininook, the Aleut people would probably have remained disparate groups, separated by distance and social differences. The spirit-mediated channels of communication that Ininook established changed all that. Shamans in bands separated by hundreds or thousands of miles communicated rapidly and efficiently, creating a new and unique unity.

It was the Aleut shaman T'singlik, born on Umnak Island, who initially claimed that all the bands who spoke the Aleut language were one tribe. At first, this claim was undeniably specious: the individual bands had very little in common, and

saw no real benefit in an affiliation wider than their own villages. This slowly changed, however, driven in large part by Ininook's application to the SAIM for official recognition of the Trans-Polar Aleut Nation. Though most members of the Aleut "tribe" would never think of themselves as such, the shamans recognized that some limited form of unity was vitally important. A military threat from "Anglo" governments never really existed, but the Aleut shamans came to fear it nonetheless, seeing unity as their best defence. T'singlik's words were passed on to other bands.

When the Anglos left, the perceived need and desire for unity quickly faded. Today, while many of the Aleut still name themselves "Aleut tribesmen," their loyalty is first and foremost to their village or their band.

The Aleut groups, particularly those on or near the Alaskan mainland, suffered the same "brain drain" in the early years of the 21st century as most other tribal groups. Young tribe members frequently turned away from their traditional upbringing and moved into Anglo "civilization." They worked as guides and "local advisors" for the oil and gas companies, helping the Anglos deal with the harsh land. Others worked as laborers, receiving technical training and academic education from the companies that hired them. When the Anglo workers left the nation, many companies decided to gamble on their Aleut employees and continue operations. The gamble paid off for a short time, but the situation was very unstable.

T'singlik had much to say to the Aleuts who had, in essence, joined the corporations by continuing to work the oil and gas rigs and the geothermal plants. He urged them to shut down those projects that were harmful to the environment. Though it took some time, his words had the intended effect. Enough Aleut workers abandoned their positions to close down the petrochemical plants.

>>>>>[In many cases, they disabled the plants beyond repair before they left.]<<<<<
—People Watcher (14:04:45/4-10-52)

The trained and educated Aleuts found themselves unable to return to their bands. After enjoying the benefits of civilization, they no longer wanted to put to sea with their fathers in seal-skin coracles to hunt whales. Instead, the vast majority moved to the Inuvik area, where those who followed Ininook were building a "cross-breed civilization," in the words of Holly T. Langland, that combined elements of traditional native culture and the most useful cultural traditions of the departed Anglos. The vast majority of the Aleut population in and around Inuvik, and all of the Aleut representation in business, comes from this successful melding of two worlds.

>>>>>[Though we couldn't return to our people and their ways, the traditions of our forefathers are still in our hearts, and we work always to maintain and strengthen them. Many of us long to return to our heritage. Those of us who feel this way call ourselves Dispossessed.]<<<<<
—Northern Light (11:03:48/3-17-52)

Many residents of the Trans-Polar Aleut Nation still wear traditional clothing, such as fur-trimmed seal-skin parkas. Traditional clothing continues to be, in many cases, more effective than modern cold-weather gear. Traditional garb is rarely seen in the cities, however, except when worn by tribal representatives visiting the seat of government.

ECONOMY

The Trans-Polar Aleut Nation has no central economy and so is not considered a true nation. Rather, it is a loosely knit affiliation of tribal and sub-tribal groups and communities subsisting mainly by hunting and fishing.

Only the Inuvik region has a national economy worthy of the name. The city of Inuvik boasts half a million residents, several large companies, and significant investment in modern technology. Several thousand hectares of the tundra area around Inuvik is covered by a large hydroponics-greenhouse project. Sub-sea companies such as Bathotech and Pisces are involved in limited sea-floor mining and drilling operations. Bathotech has purchased enough technology from the Soviets to start a pilot geothermal project on the sea floor beneath the ice cap. The amount of energy currently drawn from this geothermal plant is negligible, and it seems unlikely that the company will ever raise the capital required to make the pilot project a fully operational installation.

Inuvik's energy needs pose a significant problem. In 2039, the national government announced plans to build a fusion plant on Cape Dalhousie to supply energy to Inuvik, Tuktoyaktuk, and Alavik. The idea was scrapped in response to violent objections from many segments of Trans-Polar Aleut society. As an alternative, the government built a large solar-collector array south of Inuvik. This did little to ease the energy pinch, however, because it could only be operated six months of the year. Even when operational it was inefficient because the sun reaches such a low elevation. Inuvik is forced to purchase the majority of its power from the Athabascan Council. Superconducting lines run from a hydroelectric generating station on the Mackenzie River directly to Inuvik. In 2043, the government announced plans to dam a tributary of the Mackenzie and build its own hydro plant. This idea was killed by environmentalists who disapproved of flooding the river valley above the dam.

The Trans-Polar Aleut Nation has minimal manufacturing, and exports no manufactured products. High-technology is practically non-existent, and even Inuvik has changed little from the 1980s.

>>>>>[If you think that Danchekker's saying this is a real backwards place, you've got it. Inuvik's a hole, Tuktoyaktuk's worse, and everywhere else is pretty close to unspeakable.]<<<<<
—Blaster (01:48:24/5-1-52)

>>>>>[Tech of all kinds is expensive as drek, because it's all imported. The standard of living here bites the big one, boyo. Just check the "Facts at a Glance" section for per capita income. The figure's so low because the majority of the population survives on a hunter-gatherer or barter economy, which also explains the poverty level figure. (A word of advice: Don't tell your Inuit-on-the-street that he's poor: he'll hate you forever, and Inuit hatred makes the blackest, vilest form of hatred you'll encounter in Seattle seem like mild displeasure in comparison.) But, hey, here are the price differentials anyway:

TRANS-POLAR ALEUT COST OF LIVING	
ITEM	COST
Weaponry	
Ammunition	130% (1)*
Explosives	250% (3)
Firearm Accessories	300% (2)
Firearms	130%
Melee Weapons	70%
Projectile Weapons	80%
Throwing Weapons	70%
Armor	
Armor	280% (4)
Surveillance and Security	
Communications	150%
Security Devices	280%
Surveillance Countermeasures	320%
Surveillance Measures	250%
Survival Gear	60%
Vision Enhancers	310%
Lifestyle	
Lifestyle	150%
Electronics	
Electronics	200%+ (5)
Cybertech	
Biotech	280%
Bodyware	300%
Cyberdecks	500%+ (6)
Headware	400%
Internals	400%
Programs	400%+
Magical Equipment	
Hermetic Library	100%
Magical Supplies	40%
Magical Weapons	80%
Power Foci	50%
Ritual Sorcery Materials	60%
Spell Foci	50%
Vehicles	
Aircraft	300%
Boats	180%
Ground Vehicles	250%
Military Vehicles	— (7)

*Cost of Living Notes

(1) The wiz stuff is almost unavailable, even in the shadows. You'll even have difficulty tracking down unusual calibers of normal ammo.

(2) Everything's available in the shadows, if you know where to look, but it's all imported.

(3) Easy enough to obtain in Inuvik. Just approach any shady type from Bathotech, Pisces, and so on. Outside the Inuvik area, you just ain't gonna find it.

(4) Possession of even heavy armor is not against the law. (Why should it be? In most parts of T-PA, you'll die if you wear armor. It's not heated, after all, and it retains your body heat about as well as a negligee.

(5) Varies, depending on the sophistication.

(6) Just bring your own, chummers.

(7) T-PA has no military to speak of, and so there are no shadow sources. The UCAS has a minimal military presence, but they keep a close eye on their toys.

Magic is real cheap. The Trans-Polar Aleut Nation enjoys a strong magical tradition.]<<<<<
—The Keynesian Kid (19:17:25/2-11-52)

Smuggling, either into or out of the nation, is practically nonexistent. The reason is simple: the demand for contraband within the nation is low, and nothing produced within the Trans-Polar Aleut Nation is worth smuggling out.

>>>>>[Predictably, Danchekker passes over a very significant issue. This may not sound important, but both the Aleuts and the Inuits have an intense sweet tooth. They love sugar. This problem first appeared in the early- to mid-20th century, when the white man brought cola and chocolate to the Far North. The indigenous people had no way to produce sugar: no cane, no beets, no nothing. They developed a real taste for sweet stuff, and it grew into an addiction. The main symptom—apart from a tendency to spend nonexistent money to buy cola by the case-lot—was originally just bad teeth.

It's gotten worse. For many Inuits and Aleuts, sugar is a serious addiction. When they have access to sugar, which is still all imported, they binge. Results: hyperglycemia, manic moods, and occasional cases of acidosis like you see in unmedicated diabetics. (Additional problem: even diabetics have the addiction, and kill themselves off on a regular basis.) Addicts deprived of sugar suffer from hypoglycemia and depression. Oh yeah, and they still get bad teeth.

The government recognizes sugar addiction as a real problem. People die of sugar-induced acidosis, and steal to get money to buy "treats." (Don't let anyone tell you sugar isn't a drug. Your blood sugar level has more effect on your mood than just about anything else.) The government's first step was to slap some heavy restrictions on sugar imports.

The upshot? Sugar trafficking, of course. Smugglers can make a good living shipping sugar-rich foods or straight processed sugar into the T-PA. I know it sounds crazy, but some panzer runners stuff the vehicles to the gunwales with sugar!]<<<<<
—People Watcher (18:27:19/7-21-52)

>>>>>[Sugar runs are big money, and both the T-PA government and the smugglers treat it seriously. Three weeks back there was a major shoot-out near Alavik. The score: two T-PA national police geeked, three runners down, and a panzer blown to drek. People Watcher wasn't joking, and the smugglers sure as drek aren't.]<<<<<
—SPD (21:29:43/7-22-52)

>>>>>[T-bird run. The sweet stuff! Experienced pros only, familiar with EMCON and eyeball nav. Fax contact info and brag sheet to LTG# 3907 (24-6051).]<<<<<
—Calvin (00:18:02/6-9-52)

>>>>>[I said it in the Pueblo file, Vol. 1: this board ain't open to classified ads. I see any more like this, I purge them immediately. Get me?]<<<<<
—Captain Chaos (17:06:35/6-10-52)

GOVERNMENT

The Trans-Polar Aleut central government is a loose council of representatives from all major communities or sub-tribal groups in the nation. Each group elects a representative, who holds the position for an official one-year term. In most cases, the position is a sinecure, and the incumbent is rarely replaced. The election process varies from group to group, based on the traditions of each and the importance they attach to the position. In some groups, the election is highly formal, with official nominations and voter registration; in others, it's merely a matter of someone coming forward and expressing an interest.

>>>>>[Many sub-tribal groups and settlements don't bother sending a representative to the council at all, mainly the highly traditional groups and the isolated settlements that don't consider themselves part of any nation. They believe that if they don't send a representative, the council has no real jurisdiction over them, and that's the way they want it to stay.]<<<<<
—Nancy B (23:42:24/4-2-52)

The council meets in Inuvik on an irregular schedule. From among its members, the council elects a chief and an executive committee, who have the actual responsibility of governing the nation. The chief and committee also have the authority to hire civil servants and staff to create the infrastructure of government. Major issues must be brought before the entire council for ratification. The definition of "major" is open to interpretation, however, and the number of issues brought before the council for ratification has dropped steadily over the years. In effect, the chief and the executive committee are free to run the country as they see fit for the duration of their five-year term in office.

The chief and the committee live in official residences in Inuvik. City residences are available for the council representatives when they are in town for council meetings, but they spend most of their time in their home settlements. Council meetings are announced one week in advance, and the government is obliged to arrange transportation for council members who wish to attend.

Some sociologists claim it is impossible to govern as large, sparsely populated, and diverse a country as the Trans-Polar Aleut Nation. The actions of the nation's government seem to support their claim. The vast majority of the nation and perhaps one-third of its population are effectively without a government.

>>>>>[Not that they want one.]<<<<<
—People Watcher (22:48:27/7-21-52)

Isolated and highly traditional settlements have almost no contact with the central government. They live their lives as they see fit, taking care of their own problems, contributing nothing to the maintenance of the nation, and simply ignoring what goes on in Inuvik.

LAWS

IMMIGRATION

Immigration laws in the Trans-Polar Aleut Nation are among the strictest in North America. Non-natives are not admitted unless they have skill-sets that the government has officially recognized as needed: even Amerindians from tribes other than the Inuit and Aleut are generally unwelcome unless they meet the same criteria. This restriction is a major source of discontent in the NAN, which officially claim that all native peoples should be allowed unrestricted immigration into any tribal land. Prospective immigrants who can prove direct descent from either the Inuit or Aleut tribes are welcomed into the country and extended immediate citizenship.

Prospective non-Inuit and non-Aleut immigrants undertake a complex process when seeking approval for official immigration. First, they must apply for a job with a company based in the nation. The company approaches the government, filling out extensive paperwork proving that the applicant's skill-set is needed and currently unavailable in the nation. If the government approves this paperwork, the applicant interviews with at least two government functionaries. If the interviews go well, the government may offer the applicant immigrant status. Immigrants who enter the country by this route are never offered citizenship, however. They are classified as "landed immigrants," receiving most of the same benefits as a full citizen, but only as privileges, not rights. A landed immigrant's benefits may be revoked at any time by the government, without warning.

>>>>>[If you don't want to go through all the rigmarole, but you really want to get into the country, then a credstick with a big balance can be your best application form. But be careful: corruption exists in the government, but it isn't as widespread as in some other nations I could name.]<<<<<
—Jez (03:56:58/3-11-52)

In recent years, one faction of the council has been agitating to relax immigration restrictions. The country is drastically underpopulated, after all, and immigrants would only benefit the nation. But this faction is effectively countered by the more traditional representatives, who believe they represent a majority who are morally offended by any non-Inuit or non-Aleut immigrants.

Tourists must apply for visas from the government offices in Inuvik. Visas are valid for 28 days, renewable only from outside the country. A visa can be revoked at any time, at the discretion of any government official or member of the police force. Work visas are not available. Only citizens or landed immigrants may work in the Trans-Polar Aleut Nation.

>>>>>[You should have said "may officially work," Danchekker. We just read about how loosely the government is structured. Do you really think they're going to catch you if you hop ashore in northern Greenland and ask the locals for work?]<<<<<
—Sydney (00:19:02/7-10-52)

>>>>>[True, but who's going to hire you? And what work will you be doing? Slicing whale blubber, maybe?]<<<<<
—JoJo (12:04:41/7-13-52)

>>>>>[And don't forget how xenophobic the locals can be. Sure, you can enter the country any number of ways; the borders aren't guarded worth squat, even near Inuvik. But once you're in, you're going to find nothing but trouble.]<<<<<
—Tanis (05:03:03/7-24-52)

CIVIL AND TRIBAL LAWS

Trans-Polar Aleut national law is similar to that of the UCAS. A national Peace Force is charged with enforcing those laws, but sheer land-mass size and low population conspire to render enforcement almost impossible. The Peace Force is well trained and well equipped, normally wearing light body armor and carrying machine pistols, but the entire force numbers fewer than 500 members. Considering the overwhelming size of its jurisdiction, it is clear that enforcement would be virtually impossible if the Force tried to cover the nation evenhandedly. The Peace Force acknowledges this fact and concentrates its efforts within and around the cities of Inuvik, Reykjavik, Godth b, and Nordvik. Of these four urban centers, Inuvik is by far the best patrolled, though the enforcement level would be unacceptably low in a major UCAS city such as Seattle.

>>>>>[As a comparison, the Lone Star Security Rating lists enforcement in Inuvik as C, Reykjavik, Godth b, and Nordvik clock in at D, and the rest of the country gets the big X.]<<<<<
—SPD (03:12:32/7-24-52)

>>>>>[Gun laws are fairly well enforced in the major cities. Elsewhere, you can pack pretty much whatever you like.]<<<<<
—Bags (15:37:38/7-27-52)

>>>>>[That ain't necessarily so. Some settlements get hostile about people carrying big guns into their streets— that is, when they've got streets. They can't do much about it, but it's not a good way to make friends and influence people.]<<<<<
—Larousse (19:10:54/7-28-52)

>>>>>[Let's go back to the T-PA Peace Force. Lots of these guys are trained out-of-country. Back in 2040 or thereabouts, the government decided it would be worthwhile to send some of their peace officers to train in other nations. The T-PA set up an exchange program of sorts with the UCAS—don't ask me how— and got an infusion of some real solid skills. When that deal went sour, they set up a similar program in Athabasca. They also trained occasionally with the Sioux. It's rare, but not unheard of, to run up against a T-PA Peace Force cop who spent six months seconded to the Sioux Special Forces. The Peace boys don't usually pack much hardware, but they run on some of the slickest snow-cats, snowmobiles, and GEVs you'll ever see. When things get real dicey, they have an armory in the basement of their Inuvik barracks that would be the envy of some Lone Star detachments. I hear tell some whackos from A-M tried to break in and requisition themselves some wiz toys, but they got geeked in the process.]<<<<<
—Zip (21:54:10/8-2-52)

Individual settlement and sub-tribal group laws differ from region to region. In some areas, tribal-based taboos forbid a variety of actions ranging from drunkenness to a woman exposing her ankle. These taboos are generally enforced only through the threat of social censure or sanction.

>>>>>[Again, not necessarily so. The tribal elder in even the most out-of-the-way, god-forsaken fishing village might well be a shaman powerful enough to peel skin from bones with just a glance. Remember, the Inuit and the Aleut have a long tradition of magic. Some groups consider killing anyone who slots them around no worse than trimming a hangnail.]<<<<<
—Larousse (19:15:36/7-28-52)

INTERNATIONAL RELATIONS

Sociologists such as Holly T. Langland (*The Peoples of the North*, Electronic Arts Press, 2047) have commented that the Trans-Polar Aleut Nation seems to comprise two distinct countries. The region between the North American continent and the pole seems largely influenced, politically and socially, by the proximity of other North American nations, and belongs to the NAN. The larger part of the nation, on the other hand, feels no kinship with the other Amerindian nations and disregards anything the NAN or the NAN-aligned portion of its own nation thinks or does. The lines on the map and the country's constitution define the entire polar region as a single nation, but only the segment to the north of the continent thinks and acts like a nation. The remainder consists of an assortment of sub-tribal groups and small settlements with no cohesion and little sense of national identity.

>>>>>[Hey, fame at last! When *The Peoples of the North* was published, it only sold five copies (not enough pictures and no gratuitous sex, I figure). I know I bought four, so Danchekker must have bought the other one.]<<<<<
—Holly (12:53:59/4-12-52)

If the Inuvik region represents the Trans-Polar Aleut Nation in international relations, then the nation is on relatively good terms with most of the other NAN nations. Its closest ties are to the Athabascan Council and the Sioux Nation. The Trans-Polar Aleut government and the NAN Sovereign Council currently feel some friction over which body should ultimately define international immigration restrictions for tribal peoples, but the discussion seems to be under control.

>>>>>[Like drek. My contacts talk about an "acrimonious debate" that was close to a real donnybrook verging on physical violence in a NAN Council meeting last week. The T-PA rep, who calls herself Mary Northstar because her real name doesn't have any vowels, stormed out. The Council started talking censure, and Mary started threatening secession. Stay tuned for the next installment.]<<<<<
—Dyson (17:04:37/7-30-52)

Relations between the Trans-Polar Aleut Nation and the Algonkian-Manitoo Council are somewhat strained. The original source of the strain was a group of Algonkian elves who applied for immigration to the Trans-Polar Aleut Nation and were denied. Claiming that the southwest region of Baffin Island was their homeland, they crossed the undefended border without the nation's permission and established a small settlement near Lake Harbor that they called Ileleste, which translates as "Northhome." The Trans-Polar Aleut Peace Force mobilized and attempted to expel the settlers peacefully. When the elves fought back, killing several Peace Force officers, the situation quickly deteriorated. The Peace Force mobilized more personnel and equipment, hoping to intimidate the elves into leaving. Instead, this move strengthened the elves' resolve to stay. The settlers had several cyber-equipped ex-shadowrunners in their camp who staged several highly effective raids against the surrounding Peace Force camps. The Peace Force responded with an attempt to overrun the settlement. Even though their tactical position was untenable, the elves continued to fight. The outcome was inevitable: of the nearly 250 elves who entered the Trans-Polar Aleut lands, only 20 or so survived. The Algonkian-Manitoo government naturally denied that it had at any time sanctioned the elves' actions. Nonetheless, the "Northhome Massacre" put a lasting, severe strain on diplomatic relations between the two nations.

>>>>>[I think the real strain came from the A-M knowing that the Peace Force had their national forces outgunned. The A-M lacks good contacts among other military forces, and can't get the real wizzer stuff that T-PA imports from Sioux. That would help explain the raid on the Peace Force armory Zip talked about earlier.]<<<<<
—Jolly (11:38:35/8-5-52)

Six years ago, a good, if formal, relationship with the UCAS cooled considerably. Neither party offered an official reason, but it hardly seems coincidental that 2046 was also the year that the Trans-Polar Aleut government struck its current deal with the Sioux Nation for military training and high-technology weapons.

The Trans-Polar Aleut Nation has no diplomatic relations with any nation outside the North American continent. It recognizes no need for them.

>>>>>[What about the European States? And the SovUnion?]<<<<<
—Rackley (16:21:56/7-21-52)

>>>>>[Those countries don't consider the Inuit and Aleut worth the powder to blow them all to hell. Both the European States and the Soviet (dis)Union consider many other issues more important than playing diplomacy games with what they (wrongly) believe to be a bunch of ignorant Eskimos.]<<<<<
—Mace (01:00:16/7-29-52)

GENERAL COMMENTS

It has often been said that the majority of the Trans-Polar Aleut Nation's population would neither gain nor lose if the nation seceded from the NAN, that, in fact, they would not even notice a difference. That sentiment is, unfortunately, true.

>>>>>[But the rest of the Tribal Nations would notice. We would notice because our strength lies in solidarity. We lost something intangible and valuable when Tsimshian seceded. We can only lose again if the Trans-Polar Aleut Nation withdraws.]<<<<<
—John (21:10:24/1-27-52)

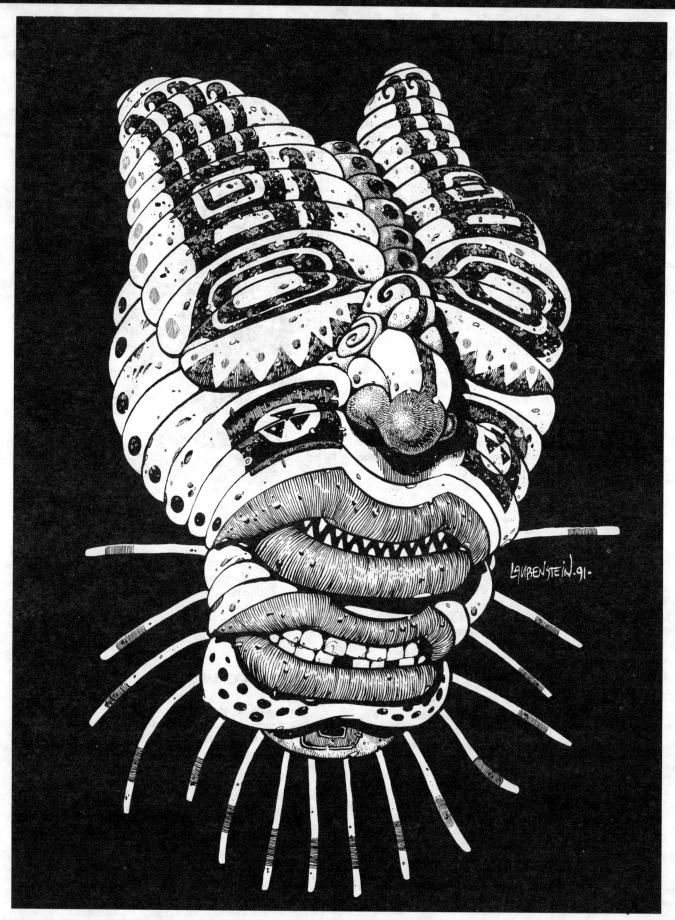

FACTS AT A GLANCE

Population: 1,050,000
    Human: 85%
    Elf: 2%
    Dwarf: 2%
    Ork: 7%
    Troll: 3%
    Other: 1%
Per Capita Income: 15,500¥
Population Below Poverty Level: 28%
On Fortune's Active Traders List: 0%
Corporate Affiliation: 12%
Education:
    High School Equivalency: 59%
    College Equivalency: 23%
    Advanced Studies Certificates: 2%
Regional Telecom Grid Access: NA/TSM

CLIMATE

The northern area of what was once British Columbia, including the Queen Charlotte Islands, and the south part of the old Alaskan "panhandle" is now the Tsimshian Nation. The prevailing winds blow in from the west almost year-round, carrying moisture picked up from the ocean. The humid winds meet the coastal mountains, cooling enough to allow the moisture to precipitate out. This weather pattern makes the Tsimshian region perpetually cloudy and rainy.

Temperatures of the mid-summer days sometimes near 20 degrees Celsius, but the nights cool off to around 10° C. Winter temperatures hover around 0° C, occasionally dropping much lower. Along with the west coast of the Athabascan Council, Tsimshian is plagued by major winter storms. High winds and heavy seas bring winter shipping practically to a stop, and safe passage is limited to the partially sheltered Inside Passage between the smaller coastal islands and the shore.

>>>>>[Like I said under Athabasca, the weather patterns around here are really hosed. Nobody seems to know why. Records from the 1990s and earlier show that the Charlottes didn't get as many real mother storms as they do now, and the cloud cover often broke during the summer for a couple of weeks at a time. Now? Forget it, chummer. Three consecutive days of sun is a heat wave, and four's a miracle. Tsimshian is a gray, depressing, wet, depressing, cold and stormy, depressing place.]<<<<<
    —Woppler the Weatherman (13:01:48/6-1-52)

>>>>>[So, Woppler, how do you like Tsimshian?]<<<<<
    —Bung (16:45:09/7-23-52)

ACCESS

Plane

One major airport serves Tsimshian, from the nation's capital of Kitimat. The runways are too short to accept suborbital or semi-ballistic flights, and so service is limited to short-haul carriers and occasional V/STOL flights. Regular service is offered between Kitimat and Vancouver, Anchorage, Juneau, Edmonton, and Calgary. From December through February, the storm season seriously curtails even this limited service.

Tsimshian Airways is the national short-hop carrier linking Kitimat with Prince Rupert, Terrace, Vanderhoof, Fort St. James, and Manson Creek, the other major cities in the nation. The storm season seriously affects this service, also.

>>>>>[Nice understatement. Since 2041, when seven—count 'em, seven—planes went down on account of storms, the TA planes stay on the ground *by law* from December 1 to February 14, and can be grounded at any other time on one-hour notice from the Kitimat weather office. (Of course, even when the weather's good you couldn't pay me enough to climb into one of those TA flying coffins.)]<<<<<
    —Sky Pilot (19:56:10/12-31-52)

Automobile or Bus

The major land routes into the Tsimshian Nation are Route 37 leading south from Watson Lake in the Athabascan Council, and Route 16 heading west from Prince George in the Salish-Shidhe Council. Route 97, then Route 12 lead south from Prince George and connect with Highway 1, which then runs southwest to Vancouver and the junction with I-5 to Seattle. Some mountain passes along these routes are completely blocked in winter, effectively isolating Tsimshian from access by land.

No bus service runs into or within the Tsimshian Nation.

Sea

In summer, the Salish-Shidhe Council runs a ferry service up the coast from Port Hardy on northern Vancouver Island to Prince Rupert in Tsimshian lands. This ferry route, which follows the scenic Inside Passage, is served by standard-hull vessels, rather than the fast multi-hull or hydroplane vessels used elsewhere in North America. This lengthens what could be a fairly quick journey to almost twelve hours' travel time. Though the ferry trip is largely intended as a tourist excursion, some business travellers and others occasionally use it.

>>>>>[Of course "others" occasionally use it. If you fly from, say, Vancouver to Kitimat or vice versa, you've got to show ID at both ends. If you take the boat, you only have to show ID when you arrive. If you arrive. Check the S-S Ferry Service confidential records sometime (not that easy, I admit, but worth the trouble). You'll see an interesting discrepancy between the number of passengers who board the ship and the number who disembark, particularly on the overnight runs. Odds are that a lot of these "missing persons" go overboard where there's nobody to see them, and make their way ashore in Tsimshian or the S-S Council. (Good to know it can be done, eh, runners?)]<<<<<
—Rox (08:20:19/4-26-52)

>>>>>[This can be more than a pleasure cruise. Two years back, a ferry got taken down by a kraken or something. No survivors.]<<<<<
—Matrix Samurai (00:20:48/8-14-52)

The Tsimshian Nation recently launched a ferry service that runs from Kitimat Harbor south to Port Hardy. The boats on this run are considerably less luxurious than those the Salish-Shidhe Council operate, however.

>>>>>[No fragging drek. You know what the fragging things are? They're the ferries the old BC Ferries Corporation used *last fragging century*. The BCFC put 'em in mothballs around 2006, but Tsimshian bought 'em and reconditioned 'em last year. And you know what takes the fragging cake? They're powered by diesel engines. That's right, chummer, fossil-fuel-burning fragging engines. Now ain't that a kick in the head?]<<<<<
—Zeppo (01:03:34/12-11-52)

>>>>>[Knock them all you want, but they get you from point A to point B, and they beat swimming.]<<<<<
—Captain Bligh (19:14:20/12-21-52)

>>>>>[So how come nobody uses them?]<<<<<
—Tailor (10:57:21/12-23-52)

>>>>>[They may not be as popular as the S-S line, but I know people do use the service. Mainly from north to south, though, which is interesting. The Port Hardy to Kitimat run must lose money because it's always almost empty. But I guess they make it up on the return trip.]<<<<<
—Captain Bligh (18:10:59/12-29-52)

TRIBAL DEMOGRAPHICS

The major tribes making up the bulk of the Tsimshian Nation are the Tsimshian, Tlingit, and Haida. The approximate breakdown of the tribally aligned population follows.

Tsimshian	55%
Tlingit	28%
Haida	13%
Kwakiutl	4%

An overwhelming majority of the total population, more than 98 percent, is tribally affiliated. When the Tsimshian Nation was formed, its leaders zealously expelled all non-Amerindians from the region. A hard-line faction of the government continues to uphold the spirit of that decision, blocking any move to allow non-natives to enter the country easily. Those few non-Amerindians who live and work in the nation are there on sufferance under the auspices of a highly restrictive work visa program. Needless to say, no pinkskin tribes have formed in Tsimshian.

Immigration restrictions against non-natives extend to Amerindian peoples not of the Tsimshian, Tlingit, Haida, or Kwakiutl tribes. When this policy went into effect, the NAN Sovereign Tribal Council denounced the restriction as repressive and voted to censure Tsimshian. The bad feelings this move engendered contributed to Tsimshian's major schism with the NAN in 2035, and its eventual official secession in 2037.

The vast majority of the nation's political power lies with the Tsimshian tribe. They hold all major governmental offices and share significant business power only with the Tlingit. Haida and Kwakiutl tribe members are second-class citizens. Haidas and Kwakiutl may only hold employment as manual laborers, and so many in these tribes are chronically unemployed. The Haida and Kwakiutl are very dissatisfied, yet seem powerless to change their circumstances.

>>>>>[Of course they've been unable to do anything about their condition. It's kind of tough when you're outnumbered almost six to one, and your oppressors control the government, civil service, police, and military. This is not to say they haven't tried. In 2041, a half-blood Haida named John George formed a radical group he called the Haida National Front. They started agitating for equal rights in the usual (political) way, and the government came down on them full force. John George went to jail along with many of his followers. The remaining members of the HNF got a little more radical—against the wishes of George, who sought a peaceful political solution to the problem—and started blowing things up. The police and the army (really the same organization) responded with brutal repression. In 2042, the cops discovered and decimated the headquarters of the HNF using Japanese-built one-man gunships they'd somehow acquired. No HNF members survived. The attack also caused lots of "secondary" casualties, but the government didn't care because the damage and deaths were limited to an exclusively Haida/Kwakiutl neighborhood. Following the military retaliation, the government put John George on trial for inciting the HNF to civil insurrection, disregarding the fact that he was incommunicado in jail at the time of the raids. He was convicted, but the court sensibly refrained from making him a martyr to the Haida/Kwakiutl cause by sentencing him to death—the standard punishment for civil insurrection. John George is still in jail, and there's no sign that he'll be released any time soon.]<<<<<
—Eagle (18:08:55/3-9-52)

>>>>>[The Haida and Kwakiutl peoples will never forget that John George sleeps on a pillow of stone for his dedication to our just and righteous cause. We will remember, we will free him—and we will avenge his persecution.]<<<<<
—Haida National Front (17:13:57/6-9-52)

>>>>>[The issue of the Tsimshian government's conduct toward the Haida and Kwakiutl, the HNF, and John George has come before the NAN Sovereign Council several times. All Council members unanimously condemn the perpetrators of this brutal repression.]<<<<<
—Wilson Gold Eagle (08:42:10/9-13-52)

>>>>>[...but since Tsimshian isn't part of your NAN any more, the STC's opinion doesn't mean drek. How about backing us with more than words, huh?]<<<<<
—Haida National Front (05:16:34/11-24-52)

>>>>>[If the Haida and Kwakiutl are second-class citizens, then non-Amerindians and members of other tribes are third class, if not lower. They're shunned, treated like dirt—even by the Haida. Sure, they're allowed to work, and they're (sometimes) paid well for what they do. But they are restricted to "visitors' en-claves"—prison camps, more like—and god help them if they ever stray outside their terri-tory.]<<<<<
—Jackson (13:13:04/12-9-52)

HISTORY AND CULTURE

The Northwest Coast region of North America historically held richer natural resources than any other area of native habitation. The ocean and rivers supplied the natives with plenty of fish and other seafood, and the thick forests, rising sharply from the beaches, offered game, edible roots, and berries. The giant redwoods, Douglas fir, and pine trees provided an endless supply of wood.

The tribes of the Northwest Coast, which included the Bella Coola, Chinook, Haida, Klikitat, Kwakiutl, Nootka, Qukleute, Qunault, Tlingit, and Tsimshian, differed from most other Amerindian tribes in that their social structure was not democratic. Each village was con-trolled by a few families that held their social position through wealth and an-cestry. These tribes measured wealth by physical possessions, especially canoes, blankets, and slaves (usually enemy warriors captured in battle). Copper, beaten into shield-shaped sheets, was the most valuable pos-session.

A tradition known as potlatch al-lowed families and individuals of high social position to display their wealth. The host of potlatch, a great feast lasting several days, invited all his family's rivals. The host-ing family gave each guest a gift, and also destroyed valuables—canoes, wooden masks,

even copper shields—to prove their great wealth. The rivals, by tradition, were required to reciprocate, forced to outdo the initial hosts at their own potlatch by destroying more wealth. Families and even whole villages could be driven to poverty by the demands of reciprocating a rival's potlatch. The modern mind quickly grasps this tradition's potential for going beyond simple self-glorification to intentionally destroy rivals.

>>>>>[If you scan later in this file, you'll see that the Tsimshian government still holds the potlatch, but in a greatly modified form. Very small gifts are given to the guests at the feast, but the government no longer destroys physical wealth. It simply can't afford to do so.]<<<<<
— Holly (15:10:17/3-10-52)

>>>>>[Not as such, Holly. But they do still destroy property sym-bolically on occasion. Remember that the old Northwest Coast tribes consid-ered slaves as part of their physical wealth? The Tsimshian annual potlatch is often the setting for the public execution of con-demned criminals. Fits, doesn't it?]<<<<<
—People Watcher (00:01:42/3-14-52)

The Northwest Coast lent itself to the native population developing a sig-nificant maritime tradition. Great seagoing canoes, some more than 20 meters long, were cut from the trunks of cedar and red-wood trees. These massive ves-sels could hold as many as 60 warriors for whale hunts and raids against enemy villages.

The Northwest Coast tribes were among the last natives to encounter the Europeans, but by 1800, fur trading flour-ished along the coast. Natives exchanged pelts with Anglo traders for iron tools, highly prized by the skilled native carvers.

The region's main art form was the huge totem poles carved from the trunks of great trees. Totem poles stood in front of nearly every home and showed the titles of the head of the household.

>>>>>[You can still find deserted villages hidden along the coast, a veritable forest of decaying totem poles seemingly sprouted in their midst. Totem carving was less extensive before the locals obtained iron tools from the fur traders. It became not so much an art as a trade.]<<<<<
—Emily (16:11:50/2-27-52)

The Northwest Coast tribes generally adapted to the European way of life. Some fishermen bought motor boats and began selling their catches to commercial packers. Other Indians took jobs in canneries or raised potatoes and other cash crops.

>>>>>[…much to our shame. We should have fought then to push the Anglos out, rather than waiting two hundred years and losing so many of our fathers' traditions.]<<<<<
—Nick Jim (17:01:58/2-24-52)

The 20th century rolled in on a tide of events that would create the Tsimshian Nation under much the same circumstances experienced by the Salish-Shidhe Council. In Canada, which encompassed the northern part of the Northwest Coast region, the laws created to answer the Amerindian question eventually led to the decline of the major tribes. "Status Indians," those who lived on registered reservations, received benefits "just for being an Indian": decreased taxation, the right to limited self-governance, even a guaranteed yearly income. An Indian who moved off the reservation lost these benefits, even if he left to take a job in the "outside world." Many older natives appreciated this attitude of Anglo consideration and clung to tradition. Many more, generally the younger, more ambitious members of the tribes, decided this was not enough. They wanted to make their own way in the Anglos' world, and gave up their government-sanctioned status to do so. Slowly but inevitably, this led to a "brain drain" in the tribes, a cultural evaporation as the young and ambitious abandoned their legal heritage. Many dominant tribes declined.

The social structure of the Northwest Coast Amerindians was focused on the band, not the tribe. Though bands belonged to tribes, individual loyalties lay primarily with the band. The land claims and environmental movements of the 1980s and 1990s were fronted by individual bands. Individual bands struggled to wrest control of their lands from the government.

Only in the latter half of the first decade of the 21st century did individual bands join together to create full-fledged tribes. Tribes pre-eminent a century and more before did not always move to the fore, however. In the Tsimshian region, the Tsimshian and Tlingit tribes led this movement, followed in influence by the Haida and Kwakiutl. Bands from other tribes still existed in much smaller numbers; however, for one reason or another they missed the boat. By the time they recognized the direction of events and organized their efforts, other tribes had consolidated their positions and held the political power in the region. Many researchers claim that this chain of circumstances caused several historically large tribes to virtually disappear. They knew their future would be decided largely without their input, and so the majority abandoned the tribal way of life forever.

Goblinization, in 2021, added a new wrinkle to the social fabric of the region. When approximately 10 percent of the population metamorphosed into orks and trolls, the proud boasts of tribal solidarity became so much hot air. Regardless of their tribal positions prior to goblinization, the newly Awakened were generally feared, even hated, by their one-time brothers. The vast majority of Awakened Amerindians in Tsimshian moved south and joined the Salish-Shidhe Council.

The Tsimshian and Tlingit tribes dominate the Tsimshian nation because they moved first and en masse.

>>>>>[Also because they didn't hesitate to use overwhelming force to seize and maintain dominance. Don't forget that, bucko.]<<<<<
—Haida Princess (11:19:04/7-30-52)

Several months before the Tsimshian Nation received official recognition from SAIM, a group of Haida bands confederated and named themselves the New Haida Nation. They applied to SAIM for official recognition alongside the Tsimshian Nation, but it was never granted. When their application was rejected, the New Haida Nation faded from the political scene.

>>>>>[Faded? FADED? They were fragging wiped out by the fragging Tsimshian and Tlingit majority. *Wiped out.* I'm talking flying lead and busted skulls, high explosives and burned villages. And why didn't the SAIM, or NAN, later on, do anything about it? Because they wanted access to Tsimshian's natural resources, and the strategically important coastal region. Fragging dreksuckers.]<<<<<
—Coastal Warrior (13:36:52/5-1-52)

>>>>>[SAIM was never able to obtain substantiated knowledge of this violent repression. Even now, little evidence exists to show that it actually happened. SAIM could not act on rumors alone. The Sovereign Council did acknowledge the unfortunate incident later, however.]<<<<<
—Coyote (20:59:01/5-1-52)

>>>>>[A fragging "resolution of approbation." I'm sure it was a great comfort to the wives and children of the slain.]<<<<<
—Coastal Warrior (15:35:46/5-5-52)

Very few Tsimshian wear traditional clothing because it is simply not practical in the modern world. A few, rare traditionalists wear conical hats woven from finely-twisted spruce roots. The vast majority of citizens wear contemporary clothing, preferring natural fabrics. They wear visible symbols of their heritage, but usually limit the display to feathers or other fetishes worn in the hair or a hatband.

Traditional handcrafts, such as detailed wood carving, are still practiced in the nation.

A TRIBE IN PERSPECTIVE: THE TSIMSHIAN

The Tsimshian tribe, referred to by some historians as the Chimnesyan Indians, was one of the richest in the Northwest Coast region. The Tsimshian subsisted almost completely on fishing and the spoils of warfare with other tribes, dwelling in small villages along the Nass and Skeena Rivers in what was the Canadian province of British Columbia. The Tsimshian were the only tribe in the region to obey tribal chiefs. All other tribes pledged their loyalty only to independent bands.

The Tsimshian lived in "long houses" built with large cedar beams and planks. A single long house housed up to seven to ten families ruled by a house chief. The house chief's identity, title, and notable deeds were often displayed on a totem pole outside the house. Wealthy chiefs enjoyed the luxury of personal servants and slaves, usually captured members of other tribes. Tsimshian society was rigidly structured, each member belonging in a fixed place in the social strata. Social position was determined by ancestry and wealth.

The Tsimshian adopted some European customs, but retained many of their own traditions. The Tsimshian was one of the few tribes to retain its native language, still spoken relatively widely at the beginning of the 21st century.

>>>>>[That they retained their language indicates how they viewed their heritage. Other tribes—and I'm speaking broadly here, so don't bother me with individual exceptions—let their language slip away. Many tribes have attempted to resurrect their language, but the attempt often requires laborious reconstruction of a language that deteriorated through disuse.]<<<<<
—Holly (16:16:10/2-14-52)

>>>>>[In some cases, linguists doubt that the "resurrected" languages have much in common with what was spoken in the region hundreds of years ago. Most languages had only an oral tradition, much of which has been lost. When you hear somebody speaking what he claims to be the original Bella Coola tongue, he probably is speaking what he thinks—or wants to believe—is the original language. Many tribes decided it would be politically expedient and good for morale to regain their "original" language. If that meant making up something that sounded legitimate, that's what happened. (Don't suggest this to an Amerindian, of course: he'll be very insulted.)]<<<<<
—Sarah Bowers (19:15:12/3-10-52)

"Tribal identity" became an issue concurrent with the land claims in the 1990s and subsequent decades. The Tsimshian were in the forefront of both movements. Their prominence was largely a function of their tribal chiefs, who served as rallying points for the tribal renaissance. Whatever the overriding reason, the Tlingit and the Tsimshian came to the fore.

>>>>>[Another very interesting possibility exists for their rapid rise to power. Evidence points to the continued existence of secret societies (mentioned later by Danchekker) dating back to the 1800s, which remained active throughout the 1900s and right up to the turn of the century. These societies, according to some sociologists, preserved the traditions and functioned as touchstones, the nuclei, if you will, around which the tribal renaissance crystallized. I'm not sure I believe it. But secret societies are a proven fact today. As I say, check out Danchekker's following comments.]<<<<<
—Holly (22:18:23/6-6-52)

The most significant Tsimshian leader was Nicholas John, born near Kitimat in the year 2000. It was he who, in collaboration with several Tlingit leaders, petitioned the newly formed NAN for membership on behalf of the Tsimshian Nation.

>>>>>[Nicholas John also ordered the brutal repression of the New Haida Nation.]<<<<<
—Bald Eagle (11:46:11/5-13-52)

>>>>>[That's never been proved, and John himself steadfastly denied it to his deathbed. If I had to pick a likely culprit, I'd name his brother, Dennis John, the war leader for the Tsimshian tribe. You'll recall that Nicholas John booted Dennis off the Tsimshian tribal council because of "irreconcilable differences in philosophy" almost immediately after another vicious clamp-down on Kwakiutl and Haida independence protests.]<<<<<
—People Watcher (23:01:36/5-20-52)

Tsimshian culture supported the secret societies common to most native cultures. As with many other aspects of their society, the Tsimshian maintained these traditions in the face of the European invasion. The secret societies most likely had shamanic roots similar to the Kachina Dancers in the Pueblo region, but hard facts are scarce.

>>>>>[That's because they were secret, you slot.]<<<<<
—Bung (16:34:06/3-9-52)

The number and influence of the secret societies among the Tsimshian today is unknown.

>>>>>[Ditto.]<<<<<
—Bung (16:34:59/3-9-52)

Based on other, known, native societies, these are probably groups of shamans dedicated to preserving the ancient traditions and passing them on to the next generation.

>>>>>[Holly, I think you'll be particularly interested in this. I've talked to a member of one of these societies that calls itself the Long House Brotherhood. They're all shamans, dedicated to rescuing the land from its abusers. Now, in the Tsimshian Nation today, who's doing most of the abusing? The government. The Long House Brotherhood's goal became changing government policy. The brethren were few, but they were powerful. You might have heard about a couple of mysterious disappearances among members of the Council for the Environment in the Tsimshian government. That's how the media portrayed the circumstances. The people involved didn't disappear, they were killed in rather blood-chilling ways (like, all their bones were torn from their bodies). According to some of my contacts, the killings could only be the work of great form spirits summoned by—any guesses? That's right: the Long House Brotherhood claims responsibility. Not publicly, of course—Bung's got it right, they're secret—but to me. Interesting, wouldn't you say?]<<<<<
—People Watcher (09:45:42/7-22-52)

>>>>>[I take it you believe this, Watcher.]<<<<<
—Holly (21:31:10/7-22-52)

>>>>>[I've got no reason not to, Holly. As you know, the Tsimshian government is notably lacking in shamanic talent. But recently, and this is confirmed, they've picked up a couple of "hired gun" shamans to start hunting for the Long House Brotherhood.]<<<<<
—People Watcher (08:19:43/7-23-52)

>>>>>[What kind of shamans would take on a contract like that?]<<<<<
—Holly (10:45:05/7-23-52)

>>>>>[There are many who would relish it, those who follow totems unknown to and unguessed at by most, hidden from even those who know something of the way of shamanic magic.]<<<<<
—Man-of-Many-Names (19:10:45/8-1-52)

ECONOMY

The Tsimshian Nation economy is resource-based. The nation owns large expanses of forest, and conducts clear-cut logging operations on an ongoing basis. Clear-cut areas must be replanted, according to Tsimshian Forestry Service law, but replanting is a low priority for the companies and is usually left undone until after erosion has already taken its toll on the land. Though Tsimshian boasts of its "scientific sylviculture techniques," the trees that grow in replanted areas are rarely as vigorous as true old-growth forest.

>>>>>[*Clear-cut logging?* In the 21st century?]<<<<<
—Tasp (16:01:12/9-28-52)

>>>>>[I know it sounds weird. But some markets around the world need wood, and Tsimshian is happy to sell its lumber.]<<<<<
—Bosko (23:10:49/9-29-52)

>>>>>[But those markets are small and getting smaller, Bosko, you apologist for tree-killers. There is no excuse for clear-cutting. The real culprit is the Tsimshian government. The logging companies receive subsidies for each hectare they cut, no matter what happens to the logs, even if they rot in the storage areas. Tsimshian cuts 50 percent more trees than it sells, and the surplus is left to decay, a waste of natural resources. The government subsidy, of course, is more than the profit to be made from cutting, marketing, and selling the trees in the first place. A logging company can make money just by logging a hillside and then leaving the logs there. If the logs sell, the company rakes in even more money. Crazy, isn't it? Crazy and criminal.]<<<<<
—Ellen Greenbough (00:37:33/11-11-52)

>>>>>[I thought Amerinds loved the land.]<<<<<
—Bundy (15:49:38/11-26-52)

>>>>>[We do. The true tribal peoples cherish the land and protect it from desecration. In that way, we Haida follow the traditions of our forefathers. The people in power in the Tsimshian Nation have forgotten this, turning away from the spiritual richness they once had. They may look native, but their hearts have become as the white man's. When John George led us, we fought for more than our own emancipation. We also fought to stop the rape of the land that is our home, our protection, and our strength.]<<<<<
—Shawnigan (21:16:22/11-28-52)

Tsimshian's economy also depends heavily on mining. Several strip mines that were first worked in the last century are still economically viable. The nation mines and smelts nickel and aluminum, two metal supplies that are severely depleted worldwide. Because some scientific and manufacturing applications still require real metal, and no satisfactory substitutes exist, prices for nickel and aluminum on the world market are high. Unfortunately, Tsimshian lacks the technology necessary to bring the mining and smelting processes to maximum efficiency. Spot prices for the metals are high, but the costs of extracting and purifying them are equally high. Tsimshian's mining industry is currently hovering around the break-even point, and conditions will only worsen as the existing mines near Terrace and Kitimat start to play out.

>>>>>[Last century, mining and smelting fragging near poisoned the land. At least with modern technology, industry doesn't choke the water and the air and burn the land. The main Kitimat smelter puts less junk into the environment than four internal combustion-engine automobiles.]<<<<<
—Bosko (08:40:06/9-30-52)

>>>>>[You've been reading the mining company's prospectus again, Bosko, you slot.]<<<<<
—Ellen Greenbough (06:45:57/10-15-52)

>>>>>[Even if the mines and the smelters are as clean as they claim—and I have grave doubts as to that—they are a blight on the spirit of the land. The land gives like a bountiful mother. It should not be raped.]<<<<<
—Shawnigan (21:22:22/11-28-52)

>>>>>[I can't believe what I'm reading. I scanned another guidebook on the area, and it said that Tsimshian left the NAN because they wanted the Sovereign Tribal Council to come down harder on the side of limiting technology.]<<<<<
—Berry (08:23:34/12-3-52)

>>>>>[Welcome to the real world, Berry, my dear. Tsimshian used that excuse (and it was an excuse, since they'd always planned to secede, at least the way I hear it), and they were convincing, because at the time they had almost no industry going. Once they were out, the government's tune changed dramatically. They needed industry to bolster their sagging economy, and said (to a certain extent) to hell with the consequences. Isn't hypocrisy wonderful? But because the guys who write guidebooks often fail to go and see what they're writing about it, they bought the "we hate technology, back to the land" line.]<<<<<
—The Keynesian Kid (18:28:26/12-5-52)

>>>>>[Many of my people found despair in their hearts at this turn of events. But what could we do? The government was too powerful, and armed resistance is not our way.]<<<<<
—Eagle Feather (21:42:09/12-13-52)

>>>>>[Maybe not yours, old man. Watch the news tomorrow to see *our* way.]<<<<<
—Haida Warrior (06:22:51/12-31-52)

The Tsimshian economy is stagnant, some even say staggering. Both the gross national product and real per capita income (adjusted for inflation) dropped at a rate of 3 percent per annum over the last five years, and the rate of decline is projected to increase. The need for increased food imports equates to a drop in the standard of living.

Tsimshian supports only primary industry. Secondary industry is scarce, and tertiary almost nonexistent.

>>>>>[In other words, tech is imported. Price differential time, chummers. Baseline Seattle, as always.

TSIMSHIAN COST OF LIVING

ITEM	COST
Weaponry	
Ammunition	130% (1)*
Explosives	150% (2)
Firearm Accessories	140%
Firearms	130%
Melee Weapons	110%
Projectile Weapons	110%
Throwing Weapons	110%
Armor and Clothing	
Armor	130% (3)
Security and Surveillance	
Communications	140%
Security Devices	140%
Surveillance Countermeasures	150%
Surveillance Measures	140%
Survival Gear	90%
Vision Enhancers	140%
Lifestyle	
Lifestyle	95%
Electronics	
Electronics	140%
Cybertech	
Biotech	150%
Bodyware	160%
Cyberdecks	450% (5)
Headware	180% (4)
Internals	180%
Programs	450%
Magical Equipment	
Hermetic Library	90%
Magical Supplies	80%
Magical Weapons	120%
Power Foci	80%
Ritual Sorcery Materials	80%
Spell Foci	80%
Vehicles	
Aircraft	140%
Boats	110%
Ground Vehicles	110%
Military Vehicles	100% (6)

*Cost of Living Notes

(1) Specialty rounds are kept under strict control by the government. (Wouldn't do to let some militant Haidas get their hooks into explosive or APDS rounds, now would it?)

(2) Explosives and mining go hand in hand, so this stuff isn't hard to track down through shadow channels. Expect to pay through the snout for forged paperwork, though (which isn't included in the price differential).

(3) Armor is restricted, even the light stuff. (Same rationale as for ammo.)

(4) Only deal with people you know, and even then, check their references real carefully. Some full-on butchers are running around out there. This applies to all cyber.

(5) Possession of a seventh-gen cyberdeck is strictly forbidden. One guy in Kitimat might be able to build one to spec (if the cops haven't gotten him yet).

(6) In other words, you'll pay a Tsimshian fixer the same outrageous commission you'd be charged in Seattle. Needless to say, the government gets a little antsy over the concept of Mr. John Q. Public cruising the streets in his very own tank, particularly when John Q. Public might be a Haida…

No big surprises, right?]<<<<<
—The Keynesian Kid (20:25:58/2-11-52)

>>>>>[The Kid once again says drek about mindbenders. BTLs are readily available, and the prices are low: maybe 80 percent of what you'd pay in Seattle. The government keeps blustering about its "war on BTLs," but nothing ever seems to change.]<<<<<
—Warpdrive (18:52:36/2-27-52)

>>>>>[That's because the government *likes* the chips coming in, particularly because most of the users are Haida or Kwakiutl. It's hard to plan civil insurrection when you're brain-fried. (Gives a whole new meaning to the phrase, "the opiate of the masses.")]<<<<<
—Jocko (04:12:32/5-3-52)

>>>>>[Are you saying the government's in the BTL-dealing business?]<<<<<
—Rabbit (06:50:41/5-3-52)

>>>>>[Not directly. It's currently handled by a Tlingit branch of the Mafia. The government just isn't putting out much heat to stop the trade.]<<<<<
—Jocko (13:14:58/5-7-52)

>>>>>[Either somebody hosed big-time, or the government's come up with a new solution to the Haida/Kwakiutl problem. Couple weeks back, a shipment of turbo BTLs came in, tainted with something nasty. So far, seven dead, three comatose, one thinks he's an orange, and four are missing (believed not having a good time). All victims were Haida or Kwakiutl. How do you scan that?]<<<<<
—Bender (08:36:55/9-22-52)

Tsimshian restricts the major multinationals to a small presence in the nation through tough enforcement of the immigration laws. Companies are free to hire non-natives as long as the company can prove to the government that the skill-set is necessary, and the new employees abide by the restrictions of their work visas, but all senior executives must be citizens of the Tsimshian Nation (i.e., Tsimshian or Tlingit; the government would never allow a Haida or Kwakiutl in a position of such power). Of course, the major corporations chafe at these restrictions. They believe, justifiably, given the average level of education in Tsimshian, that qualified executive-level employees are unlikely to be found within the nation, and that his or her loyalty to the corporation could not be guaranteed. MCT, however, has embraced this condition. The CEO of their Tsimshian subdivision is Tsimshian.

>>>>>[Here's some new buzz for you, chummers. Seems that a large deposit of manganese lies under the ocean bed just west of the Queen Charlotte Islands. Represents billions of nuyen, enough to keep the economy going for a dozen more years of mis-management. Now, Tsimshian doesn't have the tech to get at it. But MCT does. (Coincidence? The Tsimshian CEO of MCT was appointed just two weeks before the manganese find was announced. A native CEO makes MCT eligible to operate in Tsimshian. Gosh golly gee, how lucky that everything happened to work out just right.) Now MCT has the government over a barrel. MCT won't sell the government the tech it needs unless MCT gets something significant in return. I hear their asking price is a development monopoly on every area in which MCT has a major interest, and a seat on the government. Otherwise, MCT won't sell the tech and the manganese stays under a couple of hundred meters of water. The government's hanging tough at the moment, but odds are they'll eventually give in. Without that manganese and the revenue it represents, the country's going to go bankrupt in five years.]<<<<<
—The Keynesian Kid (03:50:28/12-9-52)

Tsimshian citizens are not allowed to own land. The government owns all land and leases parcels to the citizens, who act as stewards. The government has complete discretion in accepting or rejecting lease applications, and can cancel any lease on 10-days notice. Such a cancellation cannot be appealed.

GOVERNMENT

The Tsimshian Nation is nominally a democracy. In practice, however, a (somewhat) benevolent dictatorship rules. Elections are held every five years, but in the time since the country seceded from NAN, it is likely that no election has been either free or fair. The incumbent government has been in power since 2038.

>>>>>[Fixed? How? Ballot-box stuffing? Strong-arm tactics? Intimidation?]<<<<<
—Mort (21:03:27/6-20-52)

>>>>>[Nothing that blatant. Balloting is electronic, and so anyone with access to the tabulating computer can alter the results to his satisfaction. And because it's a government computer…well, you scan the rest. (And just in case any knights-in-shining-armor are thinking about it, the tabulating computer is stand-alone, not linked to the Matrix.)]<<<<<
—Flash (14:57:54/7-6-52)

Great Chief Deborah Jim has ruled the nation since 2038. The great chief selects a council of seven advisors that administers the governmental infrastructure. The nation's constitution, drawn up when Tsimshian first claimed independence from Canada, specifies that the council reflect the tribal make-up of the nation, but since 2038, the council has been exclusively Tsimshian and Tlingit.

>>>>>[I met Deborah Jim a few years back. Tiny woman, 1.5 meters tops and maybe 45 kilograms. In her early 50s, she has a face like a monkey and dresses like a corporate exec would have 50 years ago. On anyone else the costume would be laughable. But there's nothing ridiculous about dear Deborah—the very air around her crackles with will power and personality. I'd rather try to stop a bullet train with my bare hands than get between her and what she wants. She's also a highly skilled hermetic magician. (That's right, hermetic, not shamanic. I don't know why, but shamans just don't figure into the government at all.)]<<<<<
—Teddy-Boy (10:42:12/11-10-52)

>>>>>[Maybe it has something to do with what Shawnigan said earlier. To be a shaman, you've got to have a close bond with the spirit of the land, right? These fragheads don't, otherwise they wouldn't be clear-cutting and strip-mining the whole fragging countryside. Somebody with the mindset to become a shaman wouldn't do that. And if a shaman was perverted enough to be capable of raping the earth like that, then I don't think he would be able to draw on his totem any more. (But hey, maybe I'm talking drek.)]<<<<<
—Maureen (15:44:03/12-10-52)

Tsimshian has a highly efficient, uncorruptible government and civil service.

>>>>>[DREK!!]<<<<<
—Sally Steel (21:42:03/2-15-52)

>>>>>[Danchekker's right about the higher echelons. But nearer street level, Sally's got it.]<<<<<
—Aunt Acid (05:38:04/9-3-52)

LAWS

IMMIGRATION

The Tsimshian Nation enforces tough restrictions on immigration. Prospective immigrants who can show direct descent from one of the nation's four major tribes, Tsimshian, Tlingit, Haida, and Kwakiutl, may enter the country freely and receive immediate citizenship. In fact, the government has a standing offer of minor subsidies and moving allowances in an attempt to attract "acceptable" applicants from the Athabasca, Algonkian-Manitoo, and Salish-Shidhe nations.

Other tribal peoples and non-Amerindians rarely enter the country legally. Any such potential immigrant must apply to the government and prove that he or she possesses a skill-set of value to the nation. This differs from the immigration practices of other nations in that the burden of proof to show "worth" is on the applicant, not on a company wishing to employ the applicant.

>>>>>[That's the theory. In practice, it works the same as elsewhere. No non-Amerind wants to move to Tsimshian without a fragging good job waiting there. So this is the way it usually happens. A company needs someone with certain qualifications that can't be found internally. Headhunters approach a candidate and make a job offer, usually including a sweet binder/signing bonus. The headhunter makes all the necessary applications in the candidate's name, while the company back home greases a few palms. No sweat.]<<<<<
—Doc Fingers (05:32:35/1-21-52)

Only members of the nation's four major tribes may hold Tsimshian citizenship. Others who reside in the country do so under the terms of a work visa. These restrict the worker to specific visitors' enclaves, usually near the resident's work place. The enclaves are well-policed, both within and without. Unsubstantiated rumors claim, however, that police ignore visitors who leave the enclaves, even if they are victims of a crime.

>>>>>[Unsubstantiated rumors, drek. I saw it with my own eyes. Couple of toughs beating the stuffing out of some poor non-Amerindian slob while a couple of cops looked on, betting on how long it'd take the slob to go down. Got me so riled I geeked 'em all; toughs *and* cops.]<<<<<
—Hammer (17:46:37/9-4-52)

>>>>>[Just like that?]<<<<<
—Gort (07:43:31/9-7-52)

>>>>>[What'd you want me to do? Write a stinging letter of censure to my council representative?]<<<<<
—Hammer (05:31:35/9-21-52)

CIVIL AND TRIBAL LAWS

Judiciary councils head the justice system, each comprising three judges appointed by the government. The legal process resembles the adversarial system used in the UCAS, except that the judges enjoy considerably more leeway in conducting trials. A judiciary council judgment may be appealed to the great chief, but the number of reversals granted has dwindled to near none. While an appeal is officially directed to the great chief, the majority reach no further than a low-level functionary. Only the most noteworthy or newsworthy appeals actually reach the great chief's desk.

>>>>>[About once a year, Dangerous Deborah goes on the vid and publicly overturns a judiciary council conviction, usually a case along the lines of a single mother of three caught stealing bread and sentenced to four years hard time. She reverses the conviction and shakes hands with the woman, who cries with relief. The whole sideshow's a put-up job, but it's wiz PR.]<<<<<
—Tess (00:35:26/3-29-52)

Tsimshian justice sentences criminals convicted of nonviolent crimes to slavery—or, to use the accepted euphemism, "indentured service." Somewhat analogous to the "community service" sentence given in other countries, the indentured servant, or "bondsman," is assigned to a particular household or individual. Bondsmen are controlled by a surgically implanted device that rests near the brain stem. Designed like a cortex bomb, it incorporates several additional features. The fuergel explosive and detonator shares space with a small receiver keyed to a transmitter installed in the building where the bondsman works. A direct link is also made between the device and the pain centers of the bondsman's brain. An anti-tamper circuit triggers the device if any unauthorized attempt is made to remove it.

As long as the bondsman remains within a prescribed radius of the transmitter, the device is quiescent. If he moves outside that radius, but remains within a second, larger radius, the device stimulates his brain's pain centers in an agonizing reminder of the limits of his mobility. Movement outside the second radius triggers the cortex bomb. Anti-tamper circuits protect the transmitter, and will trigger the cortex bomb if the transmitter is disturbed. The person to whom the bondsman is indentured also carries a portable transmitter with two buttons. One stimulates the pain circuitry of the implant, the second detonates the explosive.

>>>>>[Fragging barbaric, uncivilized, cruel and unusual, sadistic, drek-headed, regressive practice.]<<<<<
—Randy (19:18:46/7-5-52)

>>>>>[It's worse than that. I had one of those things in my brainbox for twelve fragging months. Have you any idea how much it slots you up to know that someone can geek you at any second, any time of the day or night, just by pushing a fragging button? You get nightmares that somebody will grab you and drag you out of the safe zone just for a "joke." By the end of the year, I was really fragged in the head. I kept dreaming about taking off at a dead run, directly away from the transmitter, and just getting it over with.]<<<<<
—Harry (12:11:19/7-29-52)

>>>>>[What was your crime?]<<<<<
—Legal Beagle (14:08:53/7-31-52)

>>>>>[Fenced some vid components that fell off the back of a truck—first offense. I was out of work and my family was hungry, man. Only thing I regret is getting caught.]<<<<<
—Harry (09:40:32/8-1-52)

>>>>>[You're Haida, Harry?]<<<<<
—Holly (09:41:15/8-1-52)

>>>>>[Kwakiutl. But it's the same thing in Tsimshian.]<<<<<
—Harry (09:41:59/8-1-52)

>>>>>[One year of indentured servitude with a bomb in your brain for a first-offense "trafficking in stolen goods" charge. Sounds heavy-handed, doesn't it? Well, that's the way things are in Tsimshian. Sentences vary wildly. Harry theoretically could have got off with a small fine (and probably would have, if he'd been Tlingit or Tsimshian, of course). In general, criminal sentences hover around the average you'd expect to receive in Seattle, but range much wider around that average. (Penalties are much stiffer for anyone not Tlingit or Tsimshian.) If you'd pick up a jail term in Seattle, you'll get indentured servitude in Tsimshian. Offenses that carry a fine in Seattle might also net you the brainbomb. As a rule of thumb—but don't quote me on this, the figures vary wildly—you'd be looking at 1 to 3 months time per 1,000¥ of fine.]<<<<<
—Legal Beagle (15:33:31/8-27-52)

>>>>>[Gun laws are strictly enforced, particularly if you're non-native, Kwakiutl, or Haida. (Can't let the underclass arm themselves.) The statistics show a disturbing increase in "suspects shot while trying to escape" in gun-related busts.]<<<<<
—SPD (22:59:47/9-26-52)

The Tsimshian police force is more like a paramilitary organization, closely linked with the nation's army. Cross-training between the two forces is common, and both organizations share the same supply sources. Thus, Tsimshian police can quickly mount the firepower of an army unit if necessary. The police force has fewer than three hundred members to patrol the entire nation, but what they lack in numbers they more than make up for in determination. If the police get in over their heads, they call on the (much larger) army for support.

>>>>>[This happened during the fracas with the HNF.]<<<<<
—Roj (08:07:51/2-21-52)

>>>>>[The Tsimshian police like their armor, and they like weaponry with serious stopping power. For instance, they pack SMGs rather than machine pistols, and they routinely use APDS armor-defeating rounds. When things get nasty and they need fire-team organization, one member of the fire team carries an assault cannon. For set-piece work, they bring up belt-served 50-cals, and they have a sweet selection of belted rounds: gel (which they rarely use, since they *like* geeking people), flechette, and explosive, as well as your standard hollow-point. They're good tacticians, but a little aggressive. (The countertactic of choice is to suck 'em into a prepared free-fire zone, then pull their fangs.) In most cases, their official policy appears to be "Geek 'em first, then get fingerprints off the corpses."]<<<<<
—Hatchetman (15:36:15/2-23-52)

>>>>>[Spoken like a true razorguy. Hatchet, you're a tad predictable, but I've got to admire someone who is what he is.]<<<<<
—FastJack (13:57:13/2-27-52)

>>>>>[No kidding the army is larger. Tsimshian's army is big enough to protect a country twice its size. Officially released figures place the army at 10,000 troops, but unofficial projections are almost twice that.

They're very well equipped, though they don't advertise that fact, and only use the wiz stuff when they think they're away from prying eyes. (The wiz gear is all Japanese-built, though both Tsimshian and the Japanese government claim to have no trade ties at all. Go figure.) The number of uniformed personnel has gone up recently. I wonder if it has anything to do with Tsimshian's rather precarious economic condition? Naaahh, I'm just being cynical…]<<<<<
—Rex (16:35:33/3-18-52)

>>>>>[Check the army's tribal distribution, and you'll discover something interesting. Tsimshian and Tlingit occupy the top echelon (of course), some Haida and Kwakiutl get into the middle (junior-officer land), but the ranks are mainly Tsimshian and Tlingit. Why? Well, here's how I read it. In a position of power (i.e., brass) you want the upper class. Now, where do you put the potentially militant underclass, hm? Do you induct them, give them a bare minimum of training, and then stick an assault rifle in their hands? Probably not a good idea. But you *can* let the underclass in at the JO level. To be a junior officer requires a lot of time and effort. A willingness to dedicate so much time to training indicates that a person intends to stay in for the long haul. A long training (read "indoctrination and brainwashing") period, and rigorous psych testing is required. Induction of Haida and Kwakiutl into the officers' ranks makes sense when those factors are taken into consideration. A well-trained, fully indoctrinated Haida lieutenant is not as potentially dangerous as a Haida infantryman with basic training and a shiny new Panther cannon.]<<<<<
—Holly (02:34:54/6-23-52)

INTERNATIONAL RELATIONS

Since the Tsimshian Nation seceded, diplomatic relations with the other NAN states have been decidedly cool. As a protest against Tsimshian's restrictions on Amerindian immigration, a motion went before the Sovereign Tribal Council for the NAN to boycott Tsimshian metals, or at least penalize their export with heavy duties. The motion, though well intended, died, because almost all the NAN states import these metals exclusively from Tsimshian. Tsimshian and the Salish-Shidhe Council have the most strained relationship at the moment, mainly because the latter is concerned about the apparent military buildup taking place within Tsimshian.

>>>>>[The military buildup we're seeing really does mean something. We know that the Tsimshian economy is on the rocks because it has no real industry other than cutting things down or digging stuff up. Rumor has it there's a heavy deposit of something worth having under the ocean, but they don't have the tech to get at it. Now check the map. Just over the border in the S-S lands is Prince George, which happens to be the site of a fair bit of S-S manufacturing. The one light, and at least two medium industrial plants are so nice and clean and environmentally friendly and just so fragging efficient it must make the Tsimshian guys want to barf. And how far is it from Tsimshian land to Prince George? Maybe 150 klicks as the LAV flies. And the whole area is (relatively) undefended. Maybe I'm jumping to conclusions, but it's the only exercise I get.]<<<<<
—Rex (16:37:06/3-18-52)

>>>>>[You're not the only one jumping to those conclusions. I understand that the S-S Ranger Forces are staging a major training exercise in the Prince George/Bowren Lake area. What a coincidence!]<<<<<
—Zack (09:03:31/7-30-52)

>>>>>[Latest update. The NAN Sovereign Tribal Council sent official word to Kitimat letting Tsimshian know they would view any military adventurism against the Salish-Shidhe Council "with severe disapprobation." They also told the S-S to keep their "training exercise" away from the border so that it wouldn't be construed as a pre-emptive attack. The S-S is complying with NAN's edict. Tsimshian (predictably) has said frag all.]<<<<<
—Jolly Roger (21:34:43/11-11-52)

Tsimshian has no official diplomatic relations with Japan or any other nation.

>>>>[The key word there is "official." True, Tsimshian never receives shipments in vessels bearing the Japanese flag or with Japanese registry. But it's an open secret that Tsimshian buys tech from the land of the rising sun. (How, I don't know, since the country's almost bankrupt. I think *I* have a better credit rating. Unless, of course, certain Japanese businessmen know something that we don't about an imminent upturn in Tsimshian's fortunes. The boys in the S-S Council must be worried.]<<<<<
—The Keynesian Kid (16:43:42/9-9-52)

>>>>>[That's the easy conclusion. My contacts in CalFree propose an alternative. Japan's MITI, their governmental industry and technology division, wants the rights to the manganese offshore the Charlottes. I hear that MITI is backing Tsimshian's credit balance in return for license rights of some kind. So it doesn't necessarily mean a border war.]<<<<<
—Denver Dude (15:35:35/8-1-52)

GENERAL COMMENTS

The Tlingit are a matriarchal culture, while the Tsimshian tribe is strongly patriarchal. Surprisingly, this significant cultural difference causes no discernable friction.

>>>>>[…until and unless a Tlingit marries into a Tsimshian family or vice versa. Then there's a good chance for some kind of conflict, which is probably why it doesn't happen very often.]<<<<<
—Holly (14:30:35/8-25-52)

>>>>>[The tribes accommodate each other over sexual politics, particularly in business. When the nation originally formed and had to stand without support of the Canadian government—we're talking ancient history here—it had to put its own people in charge of business. You can imagine the problems with a Tlingit female CEO negotiating a major deal with a Tsimshian male CEO. Neither sees the other as an equal. But that's settled now, and everyone's accepted the status quo.]<<<<<
—People Watcher (21:46:12/9-1-52)

Every year on the anniversary of the country's founding, every community in the nation holds a large potlatch. The potlatch, modeled on an ancient Kwakiutl tradition (see **History and Culture**), features a salmon barbecue organized and partially subsidized by the government. Every citizen also receives a small gift from the government.

>>>>>[Each year the level of subsidy for the salmon feast and the size of the gift gets smaller as the country's economy falters. Word on the street is that the potlatch won't be held at all next year.]<<<<<
—Zip (20:43:14/9-18-52)

>>>>>[That wouldn't be a tragedy. The idea's kind of nice—warm, fuzzy, and patriotic, all that drek—but the practicality of it is something different. One segment of the population uses the potlatch as an excuse to get gooned out of its mind and tear up the place. Each year, the number of drunk and disorderly convictions increases, as do the costs of damage and the number of casualties. The cops use the potlatch as a no-penalties opportunity to beat on the minorities a little. All things considered, potlatch isn't a safe time to be abroad in Tsimshian.]<<<<<
—SPD (13:23:06/12-28-52)

Attitudes are changing, but Tsimshian remains a fairly caste-bound society, even within the upper-class tribes. Social position is very important, determined by a combination of heritage and wealth. (Thus, a poor member of a historically important family outranks a rich member of an insignificant family.)

>>>>>[The change is very slow. Currently, social position is important only in situations such as marriage, influence-peddling, and so on. Used to be that social position, more than training or aptitude, controlled a person's job choice, but this pecking order is becoming less significant all the time.]<<<<<
—Holly (20:36:22/8-25-52)

>>>>>[It's completely unimportant, unless you're at the bottom. That is, Haida, Kwakiutl, any other tribe…and worst of all, non-native.]<<<<<
—Snake (05:53:13/8-30-52)

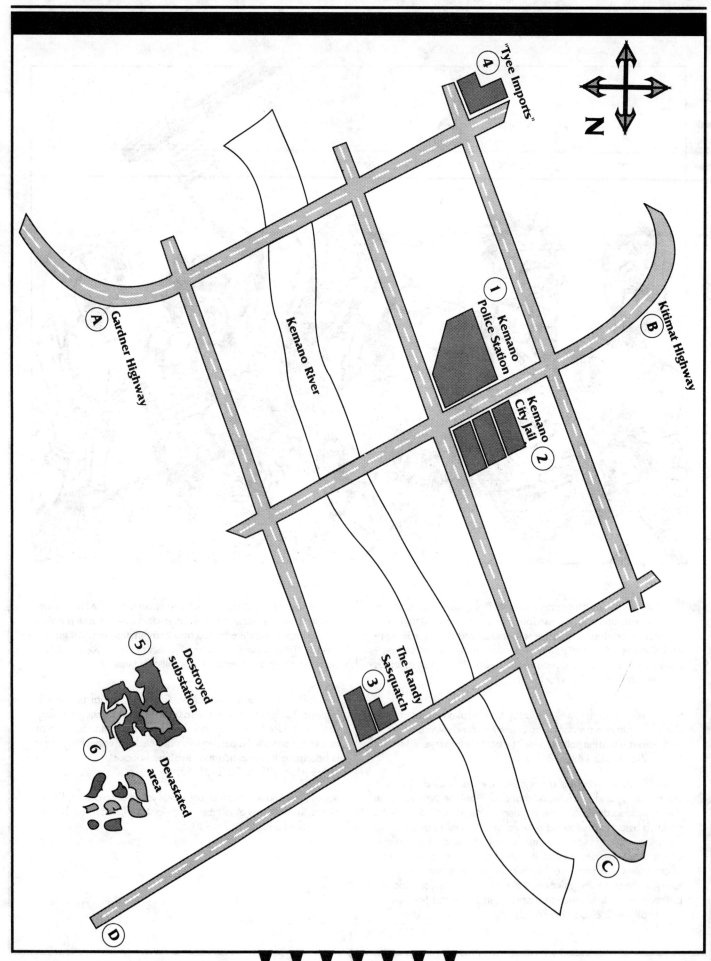

"Tyee Imports"

④

N

① Kemano Police Station

② Kemano City Jail

Ⓐ Gardner Highway

Ⓑ Kitimat Highway

Kemano River

⑤ Destroyed substation

⑥ Devastated area

③ The Randy Sasquatch

Ⓒ

Ⓓ

ATTENTION SHADOWRUNNERS!

It's a big sprawl out there and no one can see it all. Look closely at one thing and you're turning your back on something else. That's just the way it is.

We need your help. NewsNet is looking for short news articles (50 words or less) telling us what is happening as a consequence of your runs. We don't want names, we don't want events. We want only the results. Be careful, chummer, these are still shadowruns.

These articles should *not* deal with any shadowruns described in published adventures. Follow the format found in the pages of the Seattle News-Intelligencer at the back of several Shadowrun™ books.

We will publish your articles with your name in the byline in exchange for any and all rights to future use of the material. Send your articles to:

FASA Corporation
P.O. Box 6930
Chicago, IL 60680
Attn: Newsnet

SECRETS OF POWER

A SHADOWRUN TRILOGY

VOLUME ONE:
NEVER DEAL WITH A DRAGON

VOLUME TWO:
CHOOSE YOUR ENEMIES CAREFULLY

VOLUME THREE:
FIND YOUR OWN TRUTH

 SHADOWRUN™

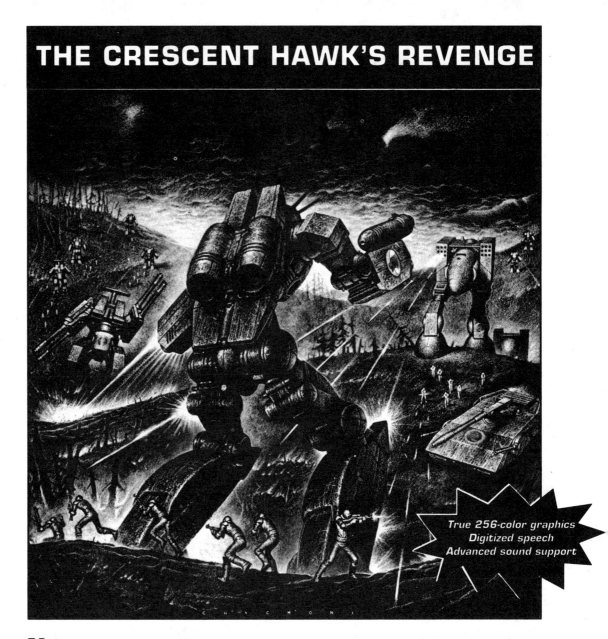

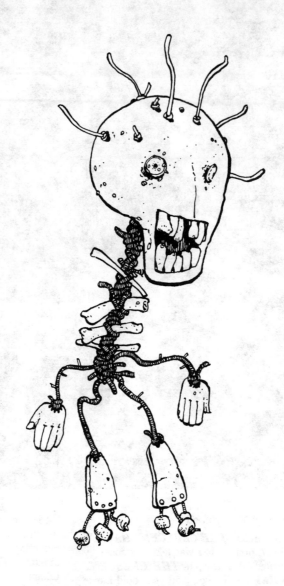

finis
▼ ▼ ▼